ALGORITHM OF YOU®

Introduction

Algorithm of You®

Emotional Algorithms: Navigating the Complex Landscape of Feelings

Introduction

Venturing into the depths of self-discovery is like navigating through uncharted waters—each wave and wind uncovers more about who we are and why we act the way we do. In this journey, you will not be following a map drawn by others, but rather reflecting on courses you have charted within yourself and empowering you to explore a concept that is at once universal and deeply personal: the emotional algorithms that guide your feelings and experiences. These are the complex systems within us that process every laugh, every tear, every heartbeat of passion, and every shiver of fear. Join us as we delve into the fascinating world of our emotions, examining the patterns and codes that influence how we interact with the world and ourselves.

Unveiling the Concept of Emotional Algorithms

Algorithm of You®

Joshua and Raena Stibal

Contents

The notion of emotional algorithms may seem foreign, a fusion of the cold logic of programming with the warm, intangible essence of our feelings. Yet it is this intricate connection that dictates your reactions and carves your unique paths through life. These emotional undercurrents are as crucial to your being as the code is to the software—it directs, it empowers, it limits, and it liberates.

Emotions, while universal in their presence, are deeply personal in their impact. They are the silent architects of your personal narratives, the unseen forces that weave the tapestry of your days. To understand how your emotions program your personal problem-solving algorithms is to unlock the power of self-awareness, to gain the clarity of why you feel a certain way when you gaze upon a masterpiece, or why your heart races in the face of danger.

In this book, we are not guiding you to merely label or list emotions; we are aiding you to dissect and comprehend them. To lay bare the framework of fears, the structure of joys, the anatomy of loves, and the shapes of sorrows. By doing so, we hope to empower you to recode, optimize, and refine your responses to the world around and within you. In this way, you can better integrate a pathway to how you experience and interact with your own life.

1

Emotions

RECOGNIZING AND NAMING EMOTIONS

Emotions are a multifaceted phenomenon, a unique conscious experience that manifests through mental states, physiological responses, and varied expressions. They are the focal point of this volume because they profoundly shape our daily existence—guiding our choices, molding our personalities, and influencing the essence of who we become. The study of emotions is not just an academic pursuit but a fascinating exploration of the brain's remarkable capabilities, offering both fun and insight into human nature.

THE COMPONENTS OF EMOTIONS

Our emotions are complex entities, composed of various elements ranging from the chemical to the experiential. Beginning with the chemical perspective, emotions are fueled by a symphony of neurotransmitters.

These include:

- Dopamine- known for its role in pleasure and motivation
- Serotonin- which impacts mood
- Noradrenaline- a driver of alertness and action
- Acetylcholine- which affects learning and memory
- Histamine- involved in our sleep-wake cycle and cognitive processes
- GABA- a key player in relaxation
- Glutamic acid- essential for synaptic plasticity

But the story of our emotions doesn't end with chemistry.

1. They also encompass cognitive appraisals- which are our mental interpretations of an event
2. Physical sensations- the bodily manifestations of our feelings
3. Action tendencies- which prime us for certain behaviors
4. Expressions- that communicate our feelings to others

The subjective experience of emotions themselves. Together, these components form the emotional algorithms that guide us through life.

Embarking on a quest to understand ourselves, we often overlook the silent whisperers of our soul: our emotions. They color every moment, yet remain elusive, often escaping our full understanding and feeling nearly impossible to convey across the multitude of communications in our lives. This section of the chapter is dedicated to the art and science of recognizing and naming our emotions. Like explorers who discover new lands, we will learn to identify the vast array of feelings that reside within us.

We'll begin by laying down the foundation:

What are emotions, and why can two people experience the same event so differently?

Emotions are complex psychological states that involve a combination of physical sensations, feelings, cognitive processes, and behavioral responses. They are typically triggered by certain events or thoughts and can influence our decision-making, perceptions, and interactions with the world around us.

The reason two people can experience the same event so differently lies in a myriad of factors that shape our individual emotional responses. These include our past experiences, cultural backgrounds, personal values, beliefs, expectations, and even our current mood or physical state. Each person has a unique emotional algorithm that interprets and reacts to events based on this intricate web of factors.

For example, while one person might feel exhilaration on a roller coaster, another might feel terror. This disparity could be due to past experiences—perhaps one has fond memories associated with amusement parks, while the other has had a frightening experience that colors their perception. Their emotional responses are filtered through their personal lenses, leading to distinct feelings about the same event. These feelings allow repeatability with each instance of emotional stimuli, aligning and providing a quicker patterned response to each roller coaster ride and providing a basis of truth for each of their individual lifetimes.

The foundation of our emotional world is built on basic emotional responses: happiness, sadness, fear, disgust, anger, and surprise. These primary emotions are universal, experienced by people across all cultures, and are often apparent even in infancy. They serve as the fundamental building blocks for more complex feelings, which evolve through a combination of personal experiences, social context, and cognitive appraisal.

For instance, happiness is a primary emotion that can give rise to feelings of joy, contentment, and satisfaction. When combined with anticipation and involvement, happiness can grow into more nuanced emotions such as optimism or enthusiasm. On the other hand, happiness mingled with elements of surprise can lead to delight or euphoria.

Similarly, the basic emotion of sadness can develop into complex feelings like grief, disappointment, or hopelessness, depending on the context and one's thought processes surrounding an event. The recognition of loss or failure might trigger sadness, which then can deepen into grief if the loss is significant or turn into disappointment if the event contradicts one's expectations.

Fear, a primal emotion vital for survival, can escalate into anxiety when we anticipate or imagine potential threats. It can also combine with other emotions to form complex responses such as jealousy, which includes elements of fear, love, and anger.

Disgust can mature into aversion or contempt, influenced by deeper evaluations of morality or personal standards. Anger, when experienced in relation to one's sense of justice, can evolve into indignation or resentment.

Lastly, surprise, while often short-lived, can lead to more complex states like shock or amazement, depending on the nature and implications of the unexpected event.

These primary emotions can mix with each other and with cognitive appraisals to form a vast array of secondary and tertiary emotions, which are more refined and specific. Understanding these basic emotions and how they develop into the varied tapestry of our emotional lives can provide invaluable insights into human behavior and our interpersonal relationships.

We may name some emotions like admiration, affection, anger, angst, anguish, annoyance, anxiety, apathy, arousal, awe, boredom, confidence, contempt, contentment, courage, curiosity, depression, desire, despair, disappointment, disgust, distrust, dread, ecstasy, embarrassment, envy, euphoria, excitement, fear, frustration, gratitude, grief, guilt, happiness, hatred, hope, horror, hostility, hurt, hysteria, indifference, interest, jealousy, joy, loathing, loneliness, love, lust, outrage, panic, passion, pity, pleasure, pride, rage, regret, relief, remorse, sadness, satisfaction, self-confidence, shame, shock, shyness, sorrow, suffering, surprise, terror, trust, wonder, worry, zeal, and zest. When we identify these emotions, we take the first step in understanding their unique hues and intensities, just as a painter must know their palette before they begin their masterpiece. Yet understand that many more combinations exist inside each person and help define how we experience the moments of our lives.

THE ROLE OF EMOTIONS IN OUR LIVES

Emotions are not just fleeting experiences; they are the undercurrent of every decision we make and every interaction we have. This section will delve into how our emotions act as guides, offering us insights into our needs, our values, and our relationships with others.

Emotions play a significant role in the formation of muscle memory, which is the process by which the brain encodes repeated physical tasks into procedural memory, making them automatic and efficient.

When an emotion is strong, especially if it is tied to an event that requires a physical response, it can enhance the learning of muscle memory. For example, the exhilaration of scoring a goal in soccer can reinforce the physical movements that led to the goal, making it easier to replicate them in the future. Similarly, the fear associated with a near miss when driving might quickly teach a driver to reflexively avoid certain dangerous maneuvers.

Positive emotions like joy, excitement, and satisfaction can boost motivation and focus, making practice sessions more effective and leading to better retention of the physical skills being learned. These emotions can also prompt the release of neurotransmitters like dopamine, which not only contribute to feelings of pleasure but also play a critical role in learning and memory.

On the flip side, negative emotions like anxiety and frustration can sometimes interfere with the performance and acquisition of motor skills. However, if managed appropriately, they can also serve as a stimulus for focused practice and improvement.

In sports, the arts, and other physical disciplines, the emotional context of training and performance can deeply influence muscle memory. Coaches and educators often aim to create a positive and emotionally charged learning environment to harness the power of emotions in developing strong muscle memory.

We will examine the dual role of emotions as both messengers and motivators. As messengers, they alert us to what is happening within our internal and external environments. As motivators, they can propel us to take action, to change course, or to remain steadfast in our path. Understanding this dual role helps us appreciate the complexity and importance of our emotional life and prepares us with the tools to harness their power effectively.

By the end of this chapter, you will not only be able to recognize and name your emotions but also begin to understand the impact they have on your daily life.

Emotions are the colors that paint the canvas of your daily experiences, influencing your thoughts, behaviors, and relationships. They are integral to your decision-making processes, your communication, and your ability to relate to others.

RECOGNIZING EMOTIONS

To begin, you must learn to recognize and name your emotions accurately. Often, we experience emotions on a spectrum, and they can be nuanced and multifaceted. A feeling of frustration might also carry shades of anger, disappointment, or even sadness. By accurately identifying these, you acknowledge their presence and can understand their origin and purpose.

We will introduce tools that help you expand on the basic emotions to include a broader range of feelings, allowing you to pinpoint your emotional state more accurately. By using this book as a guide, you will be able to distinguish between closely related emotions and label them correctly, which is the first step in understanding their impact on your life.

THE ROLE OF EMOTIONS IN OUR LIVES

Our emotions guide us, providing valuable feedback on your environment and experiences. They can act as a compass, pointing you toward your values and what matters most to you.

We will explore the function of different emotions and the way they can motivate you to take action. For instance, fear can lead to caution, which may protect you from harm, while joy can encourage you to engage more deeply with life's pleasures, reinforcing behaviors that increase your happiness.

But emotions can also be overwhelming and confusing, leading to reactions that might not align with your long-term goals. That's why we will discuss strategies for emotional regulation, such as mindfulness, deep breathing, and cognitive-behavioral techniques, which can help you to manage your emotional responses more effectively.

EMOTIONS AND DAILY LIFE

The impact of emotions on our daily lives is far-reaching. Emotions influence your relationships, your work, your communication, and your sense of self. They can affect your energy levels, your focus, and your decision-making abilities. By becoming more emotionally literate, you begin to navigate your emotions with greater ease and use them to your advantage.

For instance, when you understand that anxiety before a big presentation is a natural response, this can allow you to prepare more thoroughly and turn that anxiety into performance-enhancing focus. Similarly, recognizing the sadness behind a sense of loss can lead you to seek support and connect with others, which is crucial for healing.

Throughout this book we will provide perspective, stories, reflective exercises, and practical tips to help you apply these concepts to your own life. You will learn how to use your emotions as a source of strength and wisdom.

As we continue this journey together, remember that emotions are not just feelings to be managed but also powerful tools that, when understood, can lead to a richer understanding of yourself and the world you live in. Embrace this spectrum of emotions and let it illuminate the path to deeper self-awareness and personal growth.

2

Admiration

In this chapter, we build upon the foundation of emotional literacy established in Chapter 1 and turn our focus to a specific emotion: admiration. Admiration is a powerful, positive emotion that can serve as a catalyst for personal growth, inspiration, and connection with others. Here, we will explore the facets of admiration, share stories and reflections to deepen our understanding, and provide exercises to help identify and channel this uplifting feeling.

UNDERSTANDING ADMIRATION: STORIES AND REFLECTIONS

Admiration is often a response to witnessing excellence, virtue, or talent. It is an acknowledgment of the admirable qualities in others and can be a source of joy and motivation for the one who feels it. To understand admiration more fully, we share a narrative where admiration has played a central role in inspiring change and fostering growth. This story provides an opportunity to reflect on moments in your own life when admiration has led to pivotal decisions, the pursuit of excellence, or the deepening of relationships.

In a quaint coastal town known for its lighthouse and artistic community, there lived two individuals who, unbeknownst to them, were about to begin a journey through the multidimensional world of admiration.

Sofia, a young painter with a passion for the sea, spent her days capturing the ever-changing dance of light on the water. Her paintings were not just images, but emotions transcribed onto canvas, and they caught the eye of many. Among her admirers was Ethan, a successful businessman with no artistic bone in his body but an immense appreciation for art. He saw in Sofia's paintings a freedom and a connection to nature that his corporate world lacked.

Across the street, there was an elderly man named Mr. Jacobs, a retired sailor whose admiration for Sofia's work stemmed from a different place. In her brushstrokes, he saw the memories of his youth and the many sunsets he'd witnessed at sea. Each painting was a ticket to a time long gone and stirred a nostalgic yearning for his past adventures.

Meanwhile, Sofia harbored her own form of admiration. She was in awe of the lighthouse keeper, Thea. Her solitary life, dedicated to ensuring the safety of seafarers, symbolized a beacon of purpose and service. Sofia often painted the lighthouse, instilling a sense of guiding light in her works, much like Thea did for the ships at sea.

Thea, however, found herself admiring the very people she safeguarded. She watched from her tower as sailors maneuvered skillfully through the treacherous waters, their mastery over their vessels commanding her respect. She often thought of Mr. Jacobs, the retired sailor, as the epitome of this seafaring prowess and a living archive of maritime lore.

As the annual art exhibit approached, these threads of admiration converged. Ethan purchased one of Sofia's lighthouse paintings, feeling it represented his newfound desire to break free from his routine. Mr. Jacobs attended the exhibit, and in front of Sofia's paintings, he shared his sea tales with the town's children, his eyes gleaming with the same adventurous spirit that Sofia captured in her art.

On the exhibit's final day, Thea visited, quietly observing Sofia's rendition of her lighthouse. Seeing the emotions it evoked in viewers; Thea felt a deep connection to the community and a sense of pride in her role within it.

In the end, Sofia, inspired by Thea's dedication, unveiled a new painting. It was a homage to the sailors, the lighthouse keeper, and the sea that brought them all together. The painting depicted the lighthouse beam piercing through a storm, illuminating not just the dangerous waters but also the shared admiration between those who navigate them and those who watch from the shore.

As you reflect on this story, you have an opportunity to address how admiration can sometimes be mixed with envy or a sense of inadequacy. You may explore how to differentiate these feelings and how to transform any negative components into positive drivers for self-improvement.

EXERCISES TO IDENTIFY AND CHANNEL ADMIRATION

1. **Admiration Mapping**: Spend some time reflecting on people in your life or figures in history whom you admire. Map out the qualities that draw your admiration and explore these qualities and how they mirror any values and aspirations you hold for yourself. Is there an increased pressure on yourself to hold back, show, or use specific emotions to be seen in the same light as those you admire? Does the sense of these feelings overwhelm you, motivate you, or perhaps a different push from within your own cells?

2. **Role Model Visualization**: Visualize a person you admire and imagine a conversation with them. Ask for advice or picture their approach to a challenge you're facing. What emotions are they using to solve the situation? Are you attempting to mimic those emotion responses and force them within yourself immediately, or are you separating the approach and recognizing the differences in your own feelings and emotions?

3. **Admiration Algorithm**: Reflect and note when you experience admiration in your life. You may make mental or actual notes of instances of admiration you observe daily. This practice not only cultivates positive emotions but also helps to keep you aligned with the qualities and achievements you want to emulate. It will also help you gain a further understanding of how often you utilize and connect to the emotion of admiration.

4. **Gratitude**: Writing letters or using words to express your admiration to others can strengthen relationships and spread positive emotions. This activity includes not only

drafting such letters or speaking to those you are grateful for but also reflecting on the feelings that arise during the process.

5. **The Admiration-Action Plan**: Identify actions you can take to develop qualities you admire in others. By setting specific goals and tracking progress, you turn admiration into a tool for self-development.

As you engage with admiration through these stories and exercises, you will learn to harness the power of this emotion. Admiration can motivate you to learn, grow, and connect with others in meaningful ways. It can lift your spirits and direct your path toward becoming the best versions of yourself.

As we conclude this chapter, you can see that admiration is more than a passive experience—it is an active engagement with the world that can lead to personal transformation. Through understanding and channeling admiration, you open yourself to a world of inspiration and possibility.

3

Adoration

Building upon the foundation of emotional literacy established in the first two chapters, this chapter explores the emotion of adoration. Adoration, a step beyond admiration, is an intense feeling of regard and devotion. It's an emotion that can significantly strengthen relationships, fostering a deep sense of connection and reverence. Here, we investigate the transformative power of adoration and offer practical exercises to not only recognize but cultivate and express this profound sentiment.

THE POWER OF ADORATION IN RELATIONSHIPS

Adoration goes beyond mere appreciation; it encompasses a deep emotional investment and a cherishing of someone or something. In the context of relationships, adoration can be the glue that binds individuals together, creating a sense of belonging and mutual respect. Through stories, we will explore how adoration can elevate interactions, turning respect into a heartfelt acknowledgment of another's intrinsic value.

LUCAS

In the serene coastal town of Seabreeze Haven, nestled between the rolling waves and the whispering pines, lived a boat craftsman named Lucas. His workshop, scented with freshly planed wood and sea salt, was a sanctuary where each stroke of his planer and turn of his lathe was an act of adoration for the craft.

Lucas's reputation as a master boat builder was known far beyond the town, but to him, each boat was more than a testament to his skill—it was a vessel of life, a cradle for memories yet to be made. He saw himself as a silent custodian of the safety and joy of those who would captain his creations through the cerulean expanse.

Each morning, Lucas would stand on the shore, watching the horizon with a steaming cup of coffee warming his weathered hands. He would observe the boats dancing on the water's surface, each one a chapter in someone's adventure, a part of their journey toward discovery or homecoming. This ritual filled him with a deep sense of connection to the sea and to the sailors he served.

In his workshop, plans and blueprints were not mere guidelines but sacred texts. He selected each plank and beam with the utmost care, envisioning the families, lovers, and solitary wanderers who would entrust their dreams to the buoyancy of his craft. His hands, marked with the wisdom of his trade, moved with precision and tenderness, as if he were imbuing every inch of the hull with a silent benediction.

The townsfolk often spoke of Lucas's boats as living things. They said the vessels had a spirit, a gentle soul that made them glide through the water with an almost ethereal grace. Parents would bring their children to Lucas's dock, pointing to the boats and telling tales of the man who crafted waves into wood.

One particular creation, the *Selene*, was the embodiment of Lucas's dedication. Built for Emma, a teacher and the love of his life, the *Selene* was a vessel of shared dreams. Emma's adoration for the mysteries of sharing knowledge mirrored Lucas's own for his craft, and together, they had spent countless dusks and dawns on the *Selene*, charting stars and studying the ocean's heartbeats.

Their love story was not one of fiery passion but a tranquil, enduring flame that burned steadily, fueled by mutual respect and a shared reverence for the world around them. On the *Selene*, they were explorers, partners, and guardians of the sanctuary that was their love.

Lucas's boats, much like his love for Emma, were not just built to weather storms but to find harmony in the ebb and flow of the tides. His work was an ode to adoration itself—quiet, steadfast, and as vast as the sea. And as long as the waters whispered to the shores of Seabreeze Haven, Lucas would continue to pour his heart into the vessels that carried the souls of adventurers, lovers, and dreamers, just like him.

EMMA

In the same coastal town where Lucas crafted his boats with love and adoration, there lived Emma, a teacher whose classroom was a harbor of hope and learning. With walls adorned with colorful maps and student artwork, her classroom was a vessel of knowledge and discovery, captained by Emma's dedication to her students.

Every morning, Emma greeted each child with a smile that spoke of her deep-seated belief in their potential. She saw in their curious eyes and eager hands not just learners but future leaders, artists, scientists, and caretakers of the world they would inherit. Her heart swelled with adoration for these young minds, each as unique and full of promise as the boats that bobbed in the harbor.

Emma's lessons went beyond textbooks and tests; they were life lessons woven into stories, experiments, and explorations that ignited the children's imaginations. She taught them about the flora and fauna that thrived in their seaside environment, the tides and the winds, the stars and their stories, linking every lesson back to the life they saw around them, to the boats that sailed the horizon, and to the community they called home.

In her eyes, each challenge a student faced was a wave to be navigated, and she stood by them, a steadfast compass guiding them through academic and personal trials. When a child struggled, she was there with an encouraging word, a patient explanation, or a different approach, always seeking the spark that would light up understanding within them.

Just as Lucas infused each vessel with his soul, Emma instilled a love of learning in her students. She celebrated every small victory, whether it was a mastered math problem or a moment of kindness. Her classroom was alive with the sound of discovery, and her teaching style encompassed care and challenge, pushing her students to reach further, think deeper, and dream bigger.

Her connection with Lucas was a private source of strength. They shared a mutual adoration for their callings and for each other, each passion feeding into a shared life rich with understanding and respect. They were two halves of the same whole, united in their love for creation and cultivation—Lucas with his boats and Emma with her students.

As the school bell rang at the end of each day, Emma stood at the door, her farewells a gentle reminder of the potential she nurtured. And in the quiet of the evening, as she walked down to the docks to join Lucas on the *Selene*, her thoughts often mirrored his: thoughts of care, of purpose, and of love, knowing that the seeds of adoration she planted in her students would one day bloom into a forest of achievement and fulfillment, sailing forth on the vast sea of life.

The Storm

In Seabreeze Haven, Lucas and Emma had quietly sown seeds of adoration through their respective crafts. Lucas's boats were not mere vessels on water but carriers of communal dreams, while Emma's classroom was a nurturing ground where young minds blossomed. Together, their devotion to their work and to each other wove a strong fabric of care that enfolded their community.

One fateful autumn, a storm surged towards Seabreeze Haven, threatening to tear the fabric they had all woven. The skies darkened and the sea roared with a ferocity that sent shivers through the town. As the community braced for impact, it was that spirit of adoration, so deeply embedded in the heart of Seabreeze Haven, that became their beacon.

Lucas, with hands skilled from years of crafting strong, seaworthy boats, now worked tirelessly to fortify the town's defenses against the impending gales. He rallied a group of fishermen and townspeople, directing them with calm assurance as they reinforced docks and secured boats. His love for his craft and for the town infused his efforts with an intensity that inspired others to match his resolve.

Emma, whose affection for her students extended to their families and the broader community, organized a shelter in the school gymnasium. It became a sanctuary for those seeking refuge from the storm. Here, amidst the howl of the wind and the onslaught of rain, her calming presence soothed anxious hearts. The walls of her classroom, which had resonated with the laughter of children, now whispered comforts to all who took shelter there.

The storm raged, and the town stood firm. The adoration that Lucas and Emma had cultivated—manifested in sturdy boats and resilient spirits—held strong. As the storm subsided and dawn broke, revealing a town that had weathered the night, the people of Seabreeze Haven emerged with a renewed sense of kinship.

In the days that followed, the community came together to repair and rebuild. Lucas's workshop became a hub of activity, not just for repairs but as a gathering place for sharing stories of bravery and camaraderie from the night of the storm. Emma's classroom was filled with supplies and donations, her students eager to help those who had lost much.

The crisis had revealed the strength of the bonds forged by Lucas and Emma's adoration. It was an emotion that had transcended the personal and became the foundation for a community united in respect and care for each other. In Seabreeze Haven, adoration was more than an emotion; it was the glue that held the community together in the face of adversity. As the town healed, it was clear that the adoration they shared was not just a feeling but a force—a force as formidable as any storm and as tender as the calm that follows.

In our story set in that coastal town, the main characters, Lucas and Emma, embody the essence of adoration in their daily lives. Lucas pours his heart and soul into every vessel he builds, not just for the sake of creation but to ensure the safety and joy of those who will sail in them. Emma adores her students, recognizing the potential within each child and dedicating her life to nurturing their growth.

Their adoration for their work and the people they serve creates ripples in the community, fostering relationships built on deep respect and caring. When a crisis hits the town, it is the adoration they have sown that rallies the community to support each other, illustrating the binding power of this profound emotion.

Visualization Exercises

Visualization Exercise 1: The Tapestry of Adoration

Close your eyes and imagine yourself in a vast, quiet gallery. On the walls hang tapestries of various scenes from your life. Each tapestry is woven with threads of different emotions, but the brightest and most vibrant threads are those of adoration. As you walk along, touch the threads, feel their texture, and see where they shine the brightest. Which tapestries are most vivid? These represent the moments where adoration played a key role in your life. Reflect on how adoration influenced these experiences. Was it adoration for a person, a passion, or perhaps a pursuit? Think about how you can weave more of these brilliant threads into the tapestry of your future.

Visualization Exercise 2: The Orchard of Adoration

Envision yourself walking through a peaceful orchard where each tree bears fruit from the seeds of adoration you've planted in your life—seeds of kindness, enthusiasm, and love. Notice how some trees are bountiful and others less so, reflecting the areas of life where you've expressed more or less adoration. Reach out and take a fruit from a tree; let its flavor represent the sweetness of adoration's return in your life. Contemplate where you might plant more seeds of adoration, and visualize how you'll tend to these new trees. Feel the joy and abundance that your care and attention bring to the orchard.

Visualization Exercise 3: The Echoes of Adoration

Picture yourself standing in a valley, surrounded by tall mountains. This is the valley of your interactions with others. Call out with a voice filled with adoration and listen as it echoes back to you. Each echo represents the reciprocation of adoration from the people in your life—family, friends, colleagues. Notice the strength and warmth in the returning echoes, feel the resonance of mutual appreciation and care. How do these echoes make you feel? Which are the most powerful and why? Reflect on how expressing adoration can amplify the positivity in your relationships and how you might call out more often with this emotion in your voice.

Practical Applications: Cultivating Adoration

1. **Adoration Mapping**: Similar to the admiration mapping exercise, this involves identifying individuals or entities that evoke a sense of adoration. The difference lies in the depth of feeling—adoration is often associated with a sense of reverence and respect. Through this exercise, you will explore the deeper layers of this emotion, reflecting on what it means to truly adore.

2. **Daily Acts of Devotion**: This practical application involves small, daily gestures that express adoration, from heartfelt compliments to acts of service. The idea is to make adoration a lived experience, reinforcing the emotional bond it creates.

3. **Adoration algorithm**: Keeping a focus on moments and feelings of adoration can help to heighten awareness of this emotion and the role it plays in your life. This can include instances where you feel adored or times when you feel a strong sense of adoration toward others.

4. **Expression through Creativity**: Encourage yourself to express adoration through creative means, whether it's writing a poem, composing a song, or creating a piece of art. This activity not only celebrates the emotion but also shares its beauty with others.

5. **Reflections on Reciprocity**: Understanding that adoration is often reciprocal, you can spend moments recognizing and nurturing adoration within your relationships, emphasizing the importance of expressing and receiving this emotion openly.

As we conclude Chapter 3, it becomes evident that adoration can deeply enrich your life. It allows you to see the grandeur in the ordinary and to honor the extraordinary in a way that uplifts both the giver and the receiver. By actively engaging with and cultivating adoration, you enhance your capacity to love and to be loved, reinforcing the human need for deep, heartfelt connection.

4

Asthetic Appreciation

As we continue to strengthen our emotional literacy, Chapter 4 invites us to immerse ourselves in the world of aesthetic appreciation. This sentiment extends beyond mere visual pleasure; it encompasses a deep recognition and reverence for beauty in all its forms. It is an integral part of human experience, enriching our daily lives and influencing our well-being. In this chapter, we will explore how aesthetic appreciation manifests in everyday experiences and offer activities that will help refine our ability to perceive and savor beauty in the world around us.

AESTHETIC APPRECIATION IN DAILY LIFE

Aesthetic appreciation is often associated with the arts, but it is not confined to museums and galleries. It can be found in the mundane and the magnificent, from the symmetry of leaves and the play of shadows on a building to the thoughtful design of a well-crafted tool. This section will share stories that highlight how a cultivated sense of aesthetic appreciation can transform ordinary moments into extraordinary experiences.

MIA

In the gentle embrace of dawn, as the coastal town of Seabreeze Haven stirred awake, Mia prepared her canvas: a warm cup of freshly brewed coffee. The steam rose like morning mist as she poured the milk with a steady, practiced hand, her heart syncing with the rhythm of the waves outside her cozy café.

Each cup of coffee was an opportunity for Mia to express her aesthetic appreciation, a moment where her adoration for the art of coffee met the sleepy gratitude of her customers. Her latte art was not just a skill but a silent dialogue of beauty, a flourish that transformed a routine into a ritual, a transaction into a transfer of joy.

Today, she crafted a series of ocean-inspired designs. A frothy wave cresting over a serene sea, a delicate seashell nestled in the foam, a playful dolphin arcing gracefully amidst a whirl of cream—each one a tribute to the town's maritime spirit. Her regulars came for the rich aroma of the coffee but also for the brief immersion in artistry, for the smile that Mia's creations never failed to elicit.

For Mia, each coffee she served was a small celebration, an ode to the morning and its infinite possibilities. Her café had become a haven where art and community mingled, where every patron left with a little more lightness in their step.

As the morning rush waned, an elderly man, Mr. Jacobs, who once sailed the very seas that inspired Mia's art, settled at the counter. His eyes sparkled as Mia presented him with a latte crowned with a foam galleon, its sails billowing against the cinnamon-dusted sky. It was a tiny masterpiece that spoke of adventure and the call of the horizon.

Mia's café was a microcosm of aesthetic appreciation, a place where the love for detail and beauty was shared and savored. In Seabreeze Haven, where the pace of life ebbed and flowed like the tides, Mia's latte art was a reminder to pause and find joy in the little things, to see the world not just in its grandeur but in the intimate strokes of beauty that each day offered. Her lattes were not merely a beverage; they were an experience, a momentary voyage into the world of beauty, appreciated one sip at a time.

ALEX

In the coastal town of Seabreeze Haven, where the waves whispered secrets to the shores, Alex the architect listened with a keen ear and an open heart. His love for the town's natural beauty was not just a fleeting admiration; it was a deep aesthetic appreciation that flowed through his work, imbuing the lines and curves of his buildings with the essence of the land itself.

Alex's designs were a harmonious blend of human ingenuity and the organic elegance of Seabreeze Haven's landscapes. Each project started with a walk—a ritual of sorts—where he'd absorb the forms of the cliffs, the rhythms of the forests, and the ebb and flow of the tides. The undulating patterns of the waves, the sturdy resilience of the pine trees, and the majestic rise and fall of the coastal cliffs all whispered their wisdom to him.

His most ambitious project, a community center, was conceived as an extension of the landscape itself. The building's silhouette echoed the curves of the surrounding hills, and its expansive windows mirrored the openness of the sea. The roof arched gracefully like the waves, capturing light and shadow in a dance that changed with the hours, making the building seem alive.

The materials Alex chose spoke of the earth: stone that shimmered with the hues of the local granite, wood that carried the scent of the forests, and glass that reflected the ever-changing sky. He worked closely with local artisans, whose knowledge of time-honored techniques added depth and authenticity to the modern architecture.

When the community center was unveiled, it was as if the land had given birth to a structure that belonged there all along. The locals, who had watched the building's progress with curious and sometimes skeptical eyes, were taken aback by the way it seemed to rise naturally from the ground, as though it had always been part of the landscape.

Children played in the shadows of its walls, artists painted its myriad lights and angles, and elders sat, chatting and reminiscing, as they gazed out of the windows at the vast expanse of nature that was reflected inside.

Alex's work was a love letter to Seabreeze Haven, a tangible manifestation of his aesthetic appreciation for the place he called home. His buildings stood not as intrusions on the landscape but as tributes to it, inviting those who entered to inhabit the space but also to live in dialogue with the beauty that surrounded them. Through his vision, the town gained structures that were functional as well as poetic, each a celebration of the union between human creativity and the wild, wondrous forms of nature.

Before moving on to the visualization exercises, reflect on the story of Mia, a barista in our coastal town, whose flair for latte art brings joy not only to herself but to her customers. Her intricate designs on the foam of a morning coffee become a small celebration of beauty that enhances her customers' day. And consider the story of Alex, an architect whose appreciation for the lines and curves of the local landscape influences the design of buildings that complement and enhance their natural surroundings.

VISUALIZATION EXERCISES

Visualization Exercise 1: The Gallery of Nature

Close your eyes and imagine yourself stepping into a vast, open gallery filled with natural light. This is your personal gallery of aesthetic appreciation, displaying the most beautiful scenes you've ever encountered. As you walk through this space, observe the artworks that line the walls: majestic landscapes, intricate patterns of leaves, the delicate brushstrokes of sunset colors across the sky. With each piece, pause and reflect on the emotions they evoke. What details stand out to you? How does acknowledging these details make you feel more connected to the world? Allow yourself to absorb the beauty, letting it fill you with a sense of peace and wonder.

Visualization Exercise 2: The Sculptor's Vision

Envision yourself as a sculptor in a studio, surrounded by blocks of untouched marble. Each block represents an element of the world around you that you find aesthetically pleasing. It could be the curve of a river, the form of a cloud, or the outline of a city skyline. With tools in hand, start to chisel away, shaping the marble to reveal the form within. Feel the satisfaction as your vision comes to life, the connection between your inner world and the beauty you perceive in the external world. What emotions arise as you create? How does bringing forth this beauty reflect your understanding and appreciation of aesthetics?

Visualization Exercise 3: The Symphony of Senses

Imagine yourself seated in an opulent concert hall, the air humming with anticipation. As the symphony of life begins, each movement is a different sensory experience that you find aesthetically pleasing. The first is a visual feast, the next a tracery of touch, followed by a medley of scents, a chorus of tastes, and finally, an ensemble of sounds. Each note, each harmony, resonates with your personal sense of beauty. Observe how each sense contributes to your overall experience of aesthetic appreciation. Which sense brings you the most joy? How do these sensory experiences blend together to create a symphony of aesthetic appreciation in your life?

ACTIVITIES TO ENHANCE AESTHETIC APPRECIATION

1. **Beauty Scavenger Hunt:** By engaging in this activity, we encourage you to find elements of beauty in unexpected

places. Create a list of aesthetic elements to look for each day, such as a color, shape, texture, or pattern. In this way, you will become more attuned to the beauty that surrounds you.

2. **Mindful Observation:** Practice sitting quietly in a natural setting or a space with art, and observe the details with all senses. This exercise promotes a deeper connection with objects or scenes, allowing for a fuller appreciation of their beauty in your life.

3. **Photography Challenge:** Use a camera or smartphone to capture images of everyday beauty. This not only serves as a record of beautiful moments but also trains the eye to notice and appreciate aesthetic qualities in ordinary settings.

4. **Artistic Expression Workshops:** Engage in workshops or classes that explore various forms of artistic expression, such as painting, music, or dance. These experiences can heighten one's sensitivity to the nuances of beauty across different mediums.

5. **Beauty Algorithm – Daily Awareness and Integration:**

Integrate beauty into your daily life by observing and recording moments that strike you as particularly beautiful. This can be as simple as pausing to note the way the light filters through a window or as complex as understanding why a piece of art moves you. As you cultivate this habit, you'll not only surround yourself with more beauty but also begin to understand its profound effect on your well-being and emotional health. This ongoing practice is not just about recognition, but also about connecting to the emotion of aesthetic appreciation on a deeper level.

Through these stories and activities, Chapter 4 shows us that aesthetic appreciation is a form of emotional enrichment that can be cultivated and celebrated. By integrating practices that encourage you to notice and reflect on beauty, you open yourself to a world of wonder and enhance your quality of life. This chapter invites you to engage with your environments bringing a renewed sense of awareness, allowing the beauty of the world to become a source of joy and inspiration.

5

Amusement

In the rich mosaic of human emotions, amusement offers a lightness of being and a sparkle of joy that can brighten the dullest of days. Chapter 5 of our emotional literacy voyage celebrates the joy and lightness of amusement, exploring how this delightful emotion can infuse our lives with laughter and a sense of playfulness. We'll explore the ways amusement enhances our experiences and share techniques to welcome more of this cheerful emotion into your everyday existence.

The Joy and Lightness of Amusement

Amusement is a response to the whimsical, the surprising, and the downright funny aspects of life. It's the giggle that bubbles up at a child's innocent remark, the laughter shared with friends over a humorous mishap, or the smirk at a clever turn of phrase. In this section, we follow the story of Jasper, a street performer whose mime acts on the town's promenade evoke laughter and smiles from passersby, and Lily, a local dance instructor.

JASPER

In the small coastal town where the sea's murmur was a backdrop to daily life, Jasper, the jovial proprietor of the local curiosity shop, was the embodiment of amusement. His laughter was a familiar melody that wove through the marketplace, a sound that could draw a smile from even the most reserved passerby.

Jasper's shop was an alcove of wonder, nestled between the town's cobblestone streets and the wildflower-laden pathways. It was a place where wind chimes sang with the breeze and kaleidoscopes turned the ordinary light of day into a patchwork of colors. Each item in the shop, handpicked by Jasper himself, was an invitation to joy, a nudge to remember the lighter side of life.

But Jasper's gift for amusement wasn't confined to the walls of his eclectic haven. It spilled out into the streets, into the town, and into the hearts of those who knew him. He was known for his whimsical attire—a hat that always had a feather or two dancing in the wind, and a tie never without a splash of exuberant patterns.

The children of the town adored Jasper's impromptu magic tricks, which he performed with a wink and a nudge, turning a walk to school into an adventure. For the adults, his quips and jokes were a bright spot in their routine, a spark that could reignite the flame of childhood joy, often dulled by the day-to-day.

Jasper's story is one of a gentle kind of laughter, the sort that didn't overshadow but brightened, that didn't interrupt but invited. His presence was a reminder of the amusement to be found in every crevice of life, in the everyday balance of the mundane and the marvelous.

Every year, as the town's festival of lights approached, it was Jasper who wove the tales that accompanied the fireworks display. His voice, rich and warm, would narrate legends of the stars and the sea, each tale punctuated with an explosion of light and color, a choreography of his words with the night sky's sparkle.

In Seabreeze Haven, Jasper was more than a shopkeeper. He was the unwritten custodian of amusement, the guardian of giggles and the architect of smiles. His story was one of laughter lines and the glint of mischief in an eye, of a life lived with the lightness of a dandelion in the wind, and the depth of the ocean it floated over. Jasper's chapter is a constant reminder that life, no matter its ebb and flow, always holds room for amusement.

LILY

In Seabreeze Haven, where the ocean's rhythm set the pace of life, Lily infused her world with pure, infectious amusement. A local dance instructor, her spirit was as light and buoyant as the foam on the waves, and her laughter was a melody that seemed to echo the playful chatter of the seagulls.

Lily's dance studio was a bright, airy space where mirrors caught the shimmer of the sea and where the wooden floors were worn smooth by the tapping of feet. It was here that Lily taught the art of movement, turning exercise into expression and routine into revelry. To watch her dance was to witness joy in motion—each spin and leap a brushstroke of happiness.

Her classes were more than mere lessons; they were gatherings where the townsfolk could shed their inhibitions like overcoats and twirl in the warmth of camaraderie and shared delight. Children adored her for the funny faces she'd make as she demonstrated a pirouette, and adults respected her for the gentle way she encouraged even the most rhythmically challenged to find the beat.

The story of Lily is one of a gentle guide leading her fellow townspeople to discover the amusement waiting in their own two feet. Her own dance of life had known the occasional misstep and falter, but her resilience lay in her ability to laugh, to find the humor in her stumbles, and to rise again with a grin.

Each year, as spring breathed new life into the town, Lily organized the Seabreeze Haven Dance-Off, an event that became a highlight for locals and visitors alike. It wasn't about competition; it was a celebration, a collective exaltation of life. The event was Lily's masterpiece—a night of music, laughter, and movements both graceful and comically awkward, all embraced with equal cheer.

Lily's story is about life's dance—a dance of grace and guffaws, of elegance and elation. Her studio, filled with the echoes of laughter and the rhythm of tapping shoes, was a testament to the beauty of not taking life too seriously, of finding the amusement in the everyday pirouette, and of leading others to do the same in the grand dance of life.

Jasper's silent antics, mimicking the townsfolk going about their day, remind his audience to not take life too seriously, while Lily's playful use of language turns everyday observations into moments of shared amusement. Both bring a sense of communal joy and serve as reminders that life, despite its challenges, can be filled with moments of unexpected levity.

VISUALIZATION EXERCISES

Visualization Exercise 1: The Festival of Laughter

Close your eyes and imagine yourself entering a vibrant festival dedicated to laughter and amusement. Picture the stalls adorned with colorful banners, entertainers juggling and jesting, and the crowd's infectious giggles and chuckles filling the air. As you wander through this festival, allow yourself to be drawn to a performance that tickles your fancy. Maybe it's a comedic play, a slapstick act, or a group of clowns engaging in whimsical antics. Let yourself be carried away by the joy and silliness of the moment. Laugh freely and wholeheartedly, feeling the lightness and the release that comes with each bout of laughter. What does this laughter feel like? How does the atmosphere of joy affect your mood and thoughts?

Visualization Exercise 2: The Bubble of Mirth

Breathe deeply and envision yourself surrounded by shimmering, transparent bubbles floating gently around you. Each bubble contains a scene or memory that has brought you amusement in the past. Reach out and choose a bubble to pop, and as you do, watch the memory play out in front of you like a miniature movie.

It could be a funny moment shared with a friend, a family inside joke, or even a comical mishap that turned into a cherished story. Feel the laughter as it bubbles up inside you again, re-experiencing the humor and the happiness it brings. What specific moments come to mind? How do they color your life with joy?

Visualization Exercise 3: The Stream of Smiles

Visualize yourself sitting by a gently babbling stream in a sun-dappled forest. This stream carries not water, but a flow of amusing thoughts, images, and sensations. Dip your hands into the stream and lift them, watching as droplets of light-hearted ideas sprinkle back down, each one sparking a smile as it touches you. Let your imagination wander, coming up with playful, quirky, or absurd ideas just for the fun of it. Allow yourself to smile, chuckle, or even burst into laughter at the silliness of it all. How does it feel to indulge in this pure, uninhibited amusement? What new ideas and joyful thoughts can you take away from this stream to brighten your daily life?

TECHNIQUES FOR INVITING MORE AMUSEMENT

1. **Humor Algorithm – Cultivating Laughter and Lightness:** Invite humor into each day by taking note of the moments that make you laugh or smile. Whether it's a joke shared between friends, a playful situation, or even a humorous thought, acknowledging these instances enriches your daily life with joy and levity. This regular practice enhances your mood and opens your eyes to the lighter side of life, fostering a deeper connection to the joyful energy of humor.

2. **Laughter Yoga:** Discover the joy and health benefits of laughter yoga, a unique practice that combines laughter with yogic breathing exercises. Regular sessions encourage the body to release endorphins, the feel-good chemicals that reduce stress and boost mood. As a playful form of exercise, laughter yoga promotes a lighthearted approach to life, enhancing well-being through the power of laughter.

3. **Comedy and Improvisation Workshops:** Participation in comedy or improvisation workshops can sharpen your wit and enhance the ability to find humor in the everyday.

4. **Playful Experimentation:** Try to engage in new and playful activities that are out of your norm, such as trying a new sport, playing a board game, or engaging in a creative craft. These activities may bring about unexpected moments of amusement.

5. **Amusement in Communication:** Incorporate lighthearted comments and playful banter into your daily conversations. This can transform interactions and build a joyful connection with others.

As we wrap up Chapter 5, we understand that amusement is more than a fleeting chuckle; it is an essential ingredient in a well-rounded life. It encourages you to embrace the lighter side of your existence and share in the universal language of laughter. By actively seeking and creating opportunities for amusement, you can lift your spirits and those of others, spreading joy and helping develop a positive, connected community.

6

Anger

A nger, often misunderstood and maligned, is actually a fundamental human emotion with the potential for both constructive and destructive outcomes. In Chapter 6, we approach anger
with the intent to demystify it, to confront its roots, and to harness its energy in productive ways. This chapter will explore
strategies for recognizing anger's triggers, understanding its purpose, and channeling its power without causing harm.

CONFRONTING AND TRANSFORMING ANGER

Anger can arise from a sense of injustice, frustration, or threat,
and it often signals that something important to us is at stake. It
is a primal response that prepares us to "fight" against perceived
wrongs. However, in our modern context, the fight is rarely a
physical one. This section will share stories of individuals who
have faced their anger head-on, transforming it from a source of
conflict to a catalyst for positive change.

THOMAS

In the heart of Seabreeze Haven, where the harmonious ebb and flow of the tides whispered of balance, lived Thomas, a man whose relationship with anger was as tumultuous as the ocean during a storm. A local craftsman known for his exquisite wood-working, Thomas's creations were sought after for their beauty and the emotion carved into every piece. However, his fiery temper was equally renowned, a stark contrast to the serenity of his art.

Thomas's workshop was his sanctuary, filled with the scent of pine and the soft shavings that carpeted the floor like the aftermath of a gentle woodstorm. Yet the same hands that so deftly maneuvered chisel and lathe often clenched in frustration when a design didn't meet his impeccable standards or when the whispers of past grievances echoed through his mind.

The townsfolk often tread lightly around Thomas, their respect for his craft mingling with a cautious awareness of his ire. His anger, though, wasn't born from malice but from a deep-seated passion for perfection and an unresolved struggle with the tides of his own history—a history that included a mentor who was never satisfied and a personal life that seemed always just shy of contentment.

But Thomas's story is also one of transformation. Recognizing the toll his anger took on his relationships and his own well-being, he embarked on a journey of self-reflection and mastery over his emotions. He sought counsel, not just in moments of rage but in the stillness that followed, learning to understand the roots of his anger and how to channel it into his work without letting it spill over into his life.

With time, patience, and a commitment to change, the bouts of anger that once thundered through his days began to abate. In their place grew a newfound sense of control and a tranquility that mirrored the calm seas. His workshop, once an echo chamber for shouts of frustration, became a quiet space where only the soothing sounds of his craft could be heard.

Thomas learned to embrace the imperfections in wood, seeing them as unique characteristics that told a story, much like his own imperfections. He found solace in teaching young apprentices, sharing not just the skills of his trade but the wisdom gained from his battles with anger.

The story of Thomas illustrates the transformative power of self-awareness and the willingness to navigate through the stormy seas of anger. It's a story that mirrors the very essence of Seabreeze Haven, a place where even the most turbulent waters eventually find peace upon the shore. It's also a reminder that the same energy that fuels anger can be redirected to forge

VISUALIZATION EXERCISES

Visualization Exercise 1: The Volcano of Emotions

Close your eyes and envision yourself standing before a majestic volcano. This volcano represents your anger, powerful and potentially destructive if not understood and respected. See the lava of frustration bubbling inside, threatening to overflow. Now, visualize a safe channel you can create to direct the lava flow away from the nearby village, which represents your life and relationships. This channel is made from actions you can take to express and diffuse your anger constructively: deep breathing, communicating assertively, or engaging in physical activity. As you build this channel, feel your control and power over the anger, directing it to a place where it can do no harm. What steps did you take to build this channel? How do you feel as the lava flows safely away?

Visualization Exercise 2: The Anger Garden

Imagine yourself in a garden where every plant and flower represents a time you've felt anger. Each species shows the cause of the anger—misunderstandings as thorny bushes, unmet expectations as nettles. Walk through this garden and begin to tend to it, pulling out weeds, pruning overgrown branches, and planting new seeds of understanding and patience. As you garden, feel the anger being replaced by a sense of peace and clarity. Reflect on what each plant taught you and how tending to this garden changes your relationship with anger. How does the garden look once you've tended to it? What new plants will you introduce?

Visualization Exercise 3: The Anger Wave

Picture yourself surfing on a large wave in the ocean. This wave is your anger, and you are trying to ride it without being consumed by it. Feel the power of the wave beneath you, and recognize that while it is strong, you have the skills to ride it. With balance and focus, master the wave, using your strength and agility to stay atop. This exercise symbolizes the process of acknowledging your anger and riding through it without letting it dictate your actions. As you reach calmer waters, feel a sense of accomplishment for having managed your anger effectively. What did it feel like to stay balanced? How did you manage to ride the wave successfully?

STRATEGIES FOR HEALTHY EXPRESSION OF ANGER

1. **Mindful Recognition:** Train yourself to recognize the physical and mental signs of anger. Mindfulness can create a space between feeling anger and acting on it, providing an opportunity for choice and reflection.

2. **Anger Algorithm:** Keep a focus on instances of anger, including triggers, thoughts, and feelings. This can help you identify patterns and find more effective ways to respond to similar situations in the future.

3. **Communication Skills:** When you feel angry with someone, seize the opportunity to express your anger through "I" statements and assertive communication, which allows for voicing displeasure without blame or aggression.

4. **Physical Activity:** Find which physical outlets are ideal for you to release and channel your anger, such as exercise or engaging in a physical hobby, which can metabolize the intense energy of anger and reduce its potential for harm.

5. **Problem-Solving Techniques:** Introduce problem-solving strategies that address the underlying causes of anger. This could include negotiation skills, conflict resolution approaches, and techniques for compromise and collaboration.

As we conclude Chapter 6, reflect on the multifaceted understanding of anger you are starting to build. You are learning not to shy away from or suppress this potent emotion, but to engage with it constructively, allowing it to become a force for good in your life and in your community. Anger, once understood and expressed healthily, can be an agent for personal empowerment and social justice.

7

Anxiety

Anxiety, a complex emotion characterized by feelings of tension, worried thoughts, and physical changes like increased blood pressure, serves as a natural alert system, preparing us to face potential threats. But when persistent and unchecked, it can become a barrier to living a fulfilled life. Chapter 7 aims to decode the intricacies of anxiety, providing readers with the insight to manage its challenges and the tools to establish a more peaceful coexistence with this common emotion.

NAVIGATING THE CHALLENGES OF ANXIETY

The experience of anxiety is as personal as it is universal. This chapter will address the diverse ways anxiety manifests and influences our daily lives. We'll explore personal narratives, such as the story of Elena, a violinist whose performance anxiety threatens her love for music, and how she learns to manage these feelings to reclaim her passion and perform with confidence.

ELENA

In Seabreeze Haven, where the cadence of the ocean's waves conducted the symphony of nature, Elena, a violinist, played her heartstrings in harmony with the tides. Her music was a reflection of her soul, each note a leap above the waves of her inner sea, where anxiety often lurked like an unpredictable undertow.

Elena's home was her sanctuary, her practice room lined with shelves of carefully arranged sheet music. This was her search for order amidst the crescendos of her worries. The violin, with its curves and grace, was her vessel, guiding her through the tempest of her thoughts with melodies that spoke of both the struggle and the beauty of her journey.

Every performance was both a challenge and a liberation. The stage was her open sea, and as she raised her bow, the first wave of anxiety would crash against her resolve. Yet with each drawn note, the fog of fear dissipated, revealing the clarity of her talent and the depth of her passion. Elena's music became her lighthouse, leading her safely to the shores of applause and appreciation.

The community adored Elena not just for her virtuosic performances but for the vulnerability she shared with them. After concerts, she would speak candidly of the anxiety that accompanied her art, the silent symphony that played within her. It was a tune many knew well, resonating with their own hidden harmonies of worry.

Her solo walks on the beach became rituals of introspection and grounding. There, with the violin resting against her collarbone, she would draw her bow along the strings, the sound mingling with the sighs of the wind, composing a private concerto with the rhythm of the waves. These moments of solitude were her rehearsals for resilience, where she learned to let the bow glide with ease even as her hands trembled.

In teaching young aspiring musicians, Elena instilled more than skill; she imparted the courage to face the stage of life, encouraging them to let their emotions flow into their music, transforming fear into beauty. She taught them that the quiver in their hands could be a vibrato of strength, that a rest was not a stop but a breath, a moment to gather oneself before the next note.

The story of Elena, the violinist of Seabreeze Haven, is a sonata of highs and lows, of an artist dancing with her shadows to the rhythm of her strings. It is a tale of the quiet bravery that underlies the pursuit of beauty and the shared understanding that, sometimes, the most touching music is born from the most turbulent waters within.

VISUALIZATION EXERCISES

Visualization Exercise 1: The Forest of Serenity

Begin by visualizing yourself at the edge of a serene forest. The dense canopy above whispers of a peace that awaits. With each step into the forest, acknowledge any feelings of anxiety as mere shadows that flicker and fade among the trees. Focus on the feel of the earth beneath your feet and the fresh, clean air filling your lungs. Allow the tranquility of the forest to seep into your senses, calming your mind like the gentle touch of sunlight filtering through the leaves. As you walk deeper into the heart of the forest, visualize your worries being absorbed by the strong, ancient trees, standing as guardians of stillness. With every breath, feel your anxiety lessen, replaced by the soothing, steadfast energy of the forest around you.

Visualization Exercise 2: The Ocean of Calm

Close your eyes and imagine yourself on a tranquil beach. Before you lies an ocean of calm, its surface smooth and undisturbed. Each wave that laps at the shore brings with it a breath of relaxation, washing away the tension. Visualize yourself drawing a symbol in the sand representing your anxiety. Watch as the gentle waves reach for it, embrace it, and then pull it out to sea, leaving the sand clear and your mind at ease. Feel the warmth of the sun on your skin, the steady rhythm of the ocean in your ears, and a sense of spaciousness within you. With each wave's retreat, feel your anxiety being taken further away, leaving you centered and serene.

Visualization Exercise 3: The Balloon of Worries

Picture yourself holding a brightly colored balloon on a string. This balloon represents your anxiety—colorful, inflated, and trying to rise. Take a moment to acknowledge the size and color of your balloon, reflecting on the worries it contains. When you're ready, visualize yourself gently releasing the balloon. Watch as it floats up into the sky, getting smaller and more distant. As it ascends, feel the weight of your worries lessen. Observe the balloon as it drifts into the vastness of the sky, becoming just a speck until it disappears completely, taking your anxiety with it. Feel a sense of release and lightness in its absence as you stand firmly grounded, free from the weight of your anxiety.

COPING MECHANISMS AND MINDFULNESS PRACTICES

1. **Mindfulness Meditation:** Step into the world of mindfulness meditation, a transformative practice that anchors you in the now. Mindfulness meditation guides you to observe your current experience without judgment, whether it's a sound, a breath, or a sensation. This awareness brings a great sense of presence, quieting the restless mind and diminishing the power of anxiety's grip. By focusing on the present, you learn to make your way through worries about the past or future, finding tranquility in the simplicity of being. Through consistent practice, you cultivate a mental space where peace can flourish, even amidst life's inevitable turbulence.

Breathing Techniques

1. **Breathing Exercise 1 Diaphragmatic Breathing:** Find a comfortable place to sit or lie down. Place one hand on your chest and the other on your abdomen. Take a slow, deep breath in through your nose, letting the air fill your lungs and noticing your abdomen rise more than your chest. Hold the breath for a moment, then exhale slowly through your mouth, feeling the abdomen lower. Repeat this process for several minutes, focusing on the rise and fall of your abdomen, to help regulate your breath and signal your body to relax.

2. **Breathing Exercise 2 – Counted Breath:** This exercise aids in focus and relaxation. Inhale slowly through your nose while mentally counting to four. Keep the breath even and smooth. Hold the breath for a count of four, then slowly exhale through your mouth for another count of four. After a few rounds, try extending the count for each segment up to eight. Consistent practice of counted breath can contribute to a calmer mental state, especially during moments of heightened anxiety.

3. **Cognitive Behavioral Strategies:** Tackling anxiety can be transformative when you apply cognitive-behavioral strategies to your daily routine. Start by keeping track of moments when anxiety arises and the thoughts that trigger it. This act of recording can illuminate patterns and give insight into the thoughts that you feel might need reshaping.

Challenge these thoughts by questioning their truth. For example, if you catch yourself thinking "I can't deal with this," pause and consider a more balanced thought like "I have faced challenges before and have come through them. I have tools and strategies to manage this situation."

Experiment with your behavior, too. Consciously step into situations you might usually avoid and see what happens. You might find that the outcomes are more positive than you expected, which can slowly chip away at the foundations of your anxiety.

By repeatedly practicing these strategies, you create a mental toolkit that empowers you to confront and change the thought patterns fueling your anxiety, leading to a calmer and more confident you.

1. **Anxiety Algorithm – Recognition and Management:**
   Develop a daily practice of tuning into your body and mind
   to recognize the early signs of anxiety. When you feel worry
   beginning to rise, pause to acknowledge it without judgment. Implement grounding techniques, such as diaphragmatic breathing or mindfulness, to re-center your focus on
   the present moment. Keep a log of your triggers and the
   strategies that help to ease your anxiety. Over time, this
   practice promotes a deeper understanding of your personal
   anxiety patterns and enhances your ability to maintain equilibrium.

2. **Professional Support:** Managing anxiety is a personal
   journey, and sometimes it requires more than self-help
   strategies. It's okay to seek professional support when you
   find the challenges of anxiety overwhelming. Therapists
   and counselors are trained to help you maneuver through
   this, offering tailored strategies that respect your unique experiences and goals. Engaging with a professional can be
   the key to unlocking a deeper understanding of your anxiety
   and finding more effective ways to cope. Remember, seeking help is a sign of strength and an investment in your well-
   being.

You should now have a deeper understanding of anxiety, and a
suite of strategies to manage it. Through practical advice and compassionate insight, this chapter equips you with the skills to reduce
anxiety's impact, helping you build resilience and retain a sense of
calm in the face of life's uncertainties. It's a step toward not just
enduring anxiety but engaging with it in a way that leads to personal growth and emotional stability.

8

Awe

The emotion of awe is a powerful feeling that often arises from encounters with something grand, unexpected, or beyond our understanding. It's an emotion that transcends the self, connecting us to something larger. In Chapter 8, we take a closer look at the experience of awe and how it can be found in the vastness of the natural world, the depths of spirituality, and at the pinnacle of human achievement. We explore methods to cultivate and harness the power of awe to enrich our lives and expand our perspectives.

ENCOUNTERING AWE IN THE NATURAL AND SPIRITUAL WORLDS

Awe can shift our focus from the mundane to the magnificent, encouraging humility and a sense of wonder. This chapter shares stories of awe-inspiring moments and their lasting impact.

MAYA

In the peaceful town of Seabreeze Haven, under the canopy of the celestial ballet, lived Maya, an astronomer whose life was forever changed by a single glimpse through the lens of her grandfather's telescope. As a child, the cosmos were just distant twinkles to her, but the night she first saw the craters of the moon, the rings of Saturn, and the swirls of a distant galaxy, her world expanded. The vastness of the cosmos, with its silent grace and ancient light, unveiled a sense of awe so enduring that it charted the course of her future.

Maya's passion for the stars became her guiding constellation. She spent her nights perched at the observatory that sat on the cliff's edge, where she unraveled the mysteries of the universe for anyone who shared her sense of wonder. Her excitement was contagious; the way she described the dance of celestial bodies made even the most complex astronomical concepts feel like poetry to the listeners.

Her observatory became a place of pilgrimage for stargazers and dreamers alike. Inside, the dome ceiling opened up to unveil the theater of infinity, a stage upon which the cosmos played out its silent sonatas. As Maya guided her telescope across the heavens, her guests followed her gaze, and together, they marveled at the cosmic spectacle. The gasps of amazement and the hushed reveries that followed were the music of her evenings.

Maya's story of awe didn't just end with admiration; it was a catalyst for education and inspiration. She organized star parties for the youth, teaching them to recognize constellations, to understand the movement of planets, and to love the skies in a way she knew could fill their lives with endless curiosity and joy.

Her passion for astronomy also took her beyond the observatory's walls and into the community. She worked with local schools to develop programs that brought the wonder of the universe to children, nurturing the next generation of astronomers who would one day peer into the depths of space and find their own awe-inspiring moments.

Maya's telescope was not just an instrument for viewing the stars; it was a portal through which she invited others to journey with her across the universe. It brought the heavens a little closer to home, turning the night sky into a canvas of possibilities.

In Seabreeze Haven, Maya's story is part of the fabric of the community, a thread that runs as deep as the night is dark. It's a tale that reminds us that sometimes, all it takes is one look through a telescope to discover a new universe within and outside of us—a universe as vast as space itself and as boundless as our capacity for awe.

JONAH

In the realm of Seabreeze Haven, where the land stretched eagerly toward the heavens, Jonah, an avid hiker known for his solitary treks, found himself on a journey that would redefine his place in the world. His destination was the summit of Mount Solace, a silent giant whose peak was said to touch the very essence of the sky.

Jonah had always sought solace in the mountains, finding in their unyielding presence a challenge that called to the core of his being. The climb was steep, a relentless ascent through whispering pines and along rocky ridges where the air grew thin and the sky a deep, piercing blue.

As he climbed, the weight of life's complexities—the incessant buzz of technology, the carousel of daily obligations—fell away like leaves from autumn trees. With each step, his breath became a meditation, and the beat of his heart was a drum echoing the rhythm of the earth beneath his boots.

The final steps to the peak were the most arduous yet the most exhilarating. Jonah pushed past his limits, propelled by a force that seemed to come from the mountain itself. And then he was there, standing at the zenith of Mount Solace, a conqueror not of the land but of his own inner tumult.

The view from the peak was a canvas of awe, a 360-degree panorama that held the world below in a reverent stillness. Jonah's gaze swept over the expanse. Rolling hills gave way to dense forests, which in turn yielded to the silver thread of a river winding its way to the sea. Above, the sky was a vault of clarity, a dome that whispered of the infinite.

It was in this moment, enveloped in the serenity of unspoiled creation, that Jonah felt a deep connection to the pulse of life around him. The mountain, with its ancient wisdom, its scars and peaks, spoke of endurance and the passage of time. Jonah realized that his true priorities were not measured in the currency of schedules and screens, but in breaths taken in the presence of majesty, in the steps that brought him closer to understanding the quiet truth of existence.

As he descended, the sense of unity with nature was a flame that warmed him from within. Jonah's perception of life's priorities had been reshaped by the mountain, by the sacred dance of wind and stone. He returned to Seabreeze Haven as a more authentic version of himself, carrying the awe of the peak in his heart and the harmony of the natural world in his soul.

VISUALIZATION EXERCISES

Visualization Exercise 1: The Cosmic Canopy

Begin by finding a comfortable place to sit or lie down. Close your eyes and take a deep breath in, then slowly exhale. Now, visualize yourself lying on a grassy hill under the night sky, far from the city's glow. The stars glitter above and the Milky Way spills across the heavens like a celestial river. Feel the gentle curve of the earth cradle you. As you gaze upward, sense the vastness of the universe and your unique place within it. The stars are ancient, their light a story traveling across time to reach you. Reflect on the marvels that exist in this boundless space. What emotions stir within you as you contemplate the enormity and beauty of the cosmos?

Visualization Exercise 2: The Majesty of Nature

Imagine yourself standing at the edge of a great canyon, the air crisp and the sky a brilliant azure. Breathe in deeply and notice the scents of the earth and the vegetation. As you peer into the canyon, take in the layers of rock and history, the colors painted by time itself. See the eagles soaring above and hear the distant rush of a river below. Feel your own sense of wonder growing as you observe this natural masterpiece that has stood the test of eons. What thoughts come to mind as you witness this splendor? How does the grandeur impact your sense of self and your connection to nature?

Visualization Exercise 3: The Ocean's Embrace

Close your eyes and picture yourself walking along a deserted beach at dawn. The sand is soft and cool beneath your feet. In front of you, the ocean stretches to the horizon, many shades of blue, green, and gray, lit by the first golden rays of the sun. With each wave that rolls in, imagine a sense of awe washing over you, a recognition of the ocean's vastness and power. As the waves retreat, they leave behind patterns on the sand, a signature of the sea. Stand there for a moment and let the rhythm of the waves become your own heartbeat. How does this connection with the ocean make you feel? What insights or new understandings do you gain from this immersive experience?

EXERCISES TO SEEK OUT AND SAVOR AWE

- **Nature Immersion:** Take the time to immerse yourself in nature, whether that means watching a sunrise, stargazing, or observing the patterns of a leaf. Focus your thoughts by following your feelings and bring a mindful presence to the connection of your emotional awe. Allowing yourself the experience of these moments can begin to amplify the feeling of awe in your life.

- **Art and Music Engagements:** Seek opportunities to experience awe through art and music, such as attending a live symphony or visiting an art exhibit. Immersing yourself in the arts is a feast for the senses and the spirit. To fully engage:

Live Symphony

Arrive Early: Give yourself time to settle in and absorb the ambiance.

Read the Program: Familiarize yourself with the pieces to be performed. This background can enhance your appreciation.

Close Your Eyes: Occasionally shut your eyes to sharpen your auditory experience and feel the music.

Observe the Musicians: Notice their coordination and passion, which often tells a story beyond the notes.

Art Exhibit

Research Beforehand: A little knowledge about the artists or the exhibit's theme can deepen your understanding.

Take Your Time: Don't rush. Stand before each piece and ponder the emotions it evokes.

Sketch or Journal: If allowed, sketch your impressions or jot down thoughts in a notebook.

Reflect: After your visit, spend time reflecting on the artwork that moved you the most.

In both experiences, engaging not just with your mind but also with your heart can create a deeper connection with the art.

Awe Reflections: To engage in reflective writing about awe-inspiring moments:

Detail the Experience: Describe where and when it happened, capturing what stood out to you sensorily.

Explore Your Emotions: Note the feelings this experience evoked, like wonder or connection.

Impact on You: Reflect on how this moment changed your perspective or approach to life.

Apply Insights: Think about actions or thoughts you've adopted since and how they align with this experience.

Keep this exercise handy, revisiting it to reconnect with those powerful emotions and insights.

- **Gratitude for the Awe-inspiring:** Cultivating gratitude for the awe-inspiring moments in your daily life opens you to the beauty and wonder that surround you, often unnoticed. Start by observing the world with fresh eyes—take note of a sunrise, the pattern of a wildflower, or a kind gesture. Keep a journal to jot down these daily encounters with awe. Reflect on why these experiences resonate with you and acknowledge the feelings they stir within. This practice isn't just about recognizing awe; it's about feeling a deep thankfulness for the vast and intricate nature of life's experiences. Over time, this gratitude deepens your appreciation for the world, making you more attuned to life's marvels and the awe they inspire.

- **Awe Algorithm:** Start by setting aside a few moments each day to recall an instance that left you in awe. It could be as grand as a mountain vista or as simple as the design of a spider's web. Note this down in a dedicated Awe Journal. Make a habit of asking yourself what about this moment was awe-inspiring, and how it made you feel. Did it give you a sense of scale, of being part of something larger? Or did it instill a feeling of serenity? Observing these moments trains your mind to seek out and appreciate the sublime in the ordinary, reinforcing your connection to the world and expanding your capacity for wonder. This simple but consistent practice helps to engrain a sense of awe in your daily life, contributing to an overall richer experience of the world.

Awe has the power to inspire, to heal, and to connect you with the essence of life itself. This chapter invites you to open your heart and mind to the wonder all around, helping you develop an enduring sense of awe that can bring joy, inspiration, and a deeper connection to the world.

9

Awkwardness

A wkwardness is an emotion often characterized by a sense of discomfort or embarrassment in social situations, but it's also a universal part of the human experience. In this chapter, we examine the nature of awkwardness and how it can be not only embraced but also utilized as a tool for learning and growth. Through introspection and practice, we can transform awkward moments into opportunities for deeper self-awareness and improved social interactions.

EMBRACING AND LEARNING FROM AWKWARDNESS

Awkwardness often arises in moments of social uncertainty or when our actions don't align with social expectations. However, these moments can be powerful teachers. We'll share narratives such as that of Oliver, a once-shy teenager who learns to cope with and eventually leverage his awkwardness in social situations to forge authentic connections. We'll also meet Priya, whose experience with cultural misunderstandings leads her to a new appreciation for the diversity of social norms and the beauty of honest communication.

OLIVER

In Seabreeze Haven, where each individual's quirks were as cherished as the unique patterns of the seashells adorning its shorelines, Oliver's story unfolded. A teenager with a tangle of curly hair that often fell over his eyes, he had always felt like a puzzle piece that didn't quite fit, his shyness a cloak that was both a comfort and a barrier.

Oliver's journey through the awkward alleys of adolescence was marked by blushed cheeks and stammered words, especially when the spotlight of attention fell unexpectedly upon him. His peers, a boisterous collection of burgeoning identities, sometimes surged around him like waves, leaving him feeling adrift.

But within Oliver, there was a quiet observation, a thoughtful stillness that saw the world in a way others did not. He watched, he listened, and he learned. School projects that required group work were his most challenging shoals to navigate. Yet they also became his unexpected compass, guiding him toward the realization that his unique perspective was a gift, not a hindrance.

The turning point came during a group assignment on local history. As his classmates chattered over each other, the discussion veering off course like a boat in a storm, Oliver's voice cut through the noise with a simple, insightful observation that harnessed the chaos into clarity. His awkwardness, once a source of isolation, became the force that anchored the team.

Recognizing this, Oliver began to lean into his awkwardness, wearing it like a badge of honor. His sincerity became a beacon to others, attracting those who were tired of superficial connections and craved the kind of genuine interaction Oliver offered. He found humor in his foibles, and his laughter became a shared language, disarming in its authenticity.

In time, Oliver transformed his perceived weakness into his strongest asset. He founded a club for hobbyists where misfits like him could find solace and camaraderie. Whether it was through his passionate yet halting speeches about conservation efforts or his clumsy but earnest attempts at beach volleyball, Oliver's genuine nature drew others to him.

Oliver's story demonstrates the beauty of embracing one's inherent awkwardness and turning it into a bridge rather than a barrier. In the heart of Seabreeze Haven, his progress reminds us all that it is our quirks and idiosyncrasies that endear us to others, that authenticity is the truest form of connection, and that even the most awkward among us can steer through the tides of social interaction to find our place within our community.

PRIYA

In Seabreeze Haven, where the sea united shores and stories from across the globe, Priya's tale wove through the town's fabric like a vibrant thread from a distant land. She arrived in the coastal community carrying the heritage of her ancestors, a rich assortment of traditions and customs that painted her world in vivid hues of diversity.

From the beginning, Priya found herself struggling to understand the delicate dance of cultural nuances. Her gestures of greeting, the spices and aromas that wafted from her kitchen, and the melodies of her native language often met with curious glances and hesitant smiles. The silent symphony of unspoken social cues sometimes played a tune she couldn't quite follow, leading to moments of endearing misunderstandings.

One day, while hosting a dinner for her neighbors, Priya noticed the polite puzzlement at the ritual she performed before the meal—a traditional blessing, spoken with a reverence that transcended language. The awkward silence that followed was a space where barriers grew, but also where bridges began to form.

Recognizing this moment as an opportunity, Priya embraced the awkwardness with a gracious heart. She began to share stories of her homeland, of the significance behind each dish, and the customs that were as natural to her as breathing. Her openness allowed her to illuminate the paths between cultures, and her willingness to communicate, to invite others into her world, sowed seeds of understanding.

In classrooms and community centers, Priya began to offer workshops on cross-cultural communication, transforming her once-awkward encounters into interactive sessions that celebrated the diversity of human experience. Each class was a journey into the heart of another culture, breaking down walls not with force, but with the gentle touch of genuine curiosity and the shared laughter of recognition.

Priya's story became one of transformation as she moved from the awkwardness of cultural dissonance to the symphony of multicultural harmony. Her initial experiences, once fraught with missteps, became the foundation upon which she built her mission: to create a space where the diversity of social norms was not just tolerated but cherished, and where honest communication was seen not as a cause for embarrassment but as the key to collective enrichment.

In the end, Priya's influence rippled through Seabreeze Haven as the town grew to embody a community where every individual, no matter their background, could find common ground in the universal language of humanity. Her legacy was one of laughter shared across tables, stories exchanged over cups of tea, and the understanding that awkward moments could be the starting points for the most beautiful of human connections.

VISUALIZATION EXERCISES

Visualization Exercise 1: The Mixer of Misunderstandings

Close your eyes and picture yourself at a social mixer where everyone seems to speak a different social language. Feel the initial hesitation as you approach a group, the first flutters of awkwardness. Now, visualize yourself taking a deep breath and joining the conversation with a genuine smile. As you endure the initial discomfort, see yourself finding common ground, sharing stories, and learning from the variety of experiences. With each interaction, feel the walls of awkwardness crumbling, replaced by bridges of laughter and shared human connection. What do you learn from these interactions? How does the initial awkwardness transform into a deeper understanding of others?

Visualization Exercise 2: The Dance of Cultural Celebration

Envision yourself entering a room where a cultural celebration is taking place, filled with customs and traditions unfamiliar to you. At first, you feel out of place; there are rhythms you don't recognize, dances you don't know. But as you observe and participate, you become part of the celebration, clumsily at first, then with increasing confidence. Imagine the joy and connection as you embrace the diversity around you, turning awkwardness into an opportunity to celebrate the richness of different cultures. How does this new understanding shape your perception of the world?

Visualization Exercise 3: The Speech Bubble Challenge

Imagine yourself in a scenario where you must communicate an important message, but every time you speak, the words come out in speech bubbles that are jumbled and out of order. At first, this miscommunication causes confusion and a sense of awkwardness both for you and the listener. But then, visualize yourself and the listener working together to rearrange the bubbles, finding humor in the situation and bonding over the challenge. Through this playful problem-solving, see how the initial awkwardness turns into a collaborative and enjoyable experience. How does this shared effort enhance the connection between you and the listener?

REFLECTIVE PROMPTS FOR SOCIAL SITUATIONS

- **Self-Compassion Exercises:** Self-compassion is an essential salve for the moments when we find ourselves floundering in awkward situations. It's vital to remember that such moments are a universal part of the human condition; none of us are immune. When awkwardness arises, it's an opportunity to practice self-kindness. Begin by taking a deep breath and acknowledging your feelings without judgment. Offer yourself the same empathy and understanding you'd extend to a good friend in a similar predicament. Remind yourself that perfection is not the goal—growth is. Engage in exercises such as writing a letter to yourself from the perspective of a compassionate friend or creating affirmations that reinforce your worth beyond social comfort. Regularly incorporating these self-compassion exercises not only softens the sting of awkwardness but also strengthens emotional resilience, fostering a more forgiving and nurturing inner dialogue.

• **Role-Play Scenarios:** Role-play scenarios are practical tools for anticipating and navigating the common yet often daunting social interactions that can cause awkwardness. Picture yourself at a bustling networking event or sitting across from someone on a first date. By role-playing these scenarios in a safe environment, you can mentally rehearse your responses, body language, and even your exit strategies. Consider different outcomes and plan your approach: How will you introduce yourself, share your interests, or express your enjoyment? Perhaps practice active listening and asking open-ended questions that foster engaging conversations. Reflect on these rehearsals to identify and mitigate potential anxieties. Such preparation not only eases the immediate tension of the real-life encounter but also builds a foundation of confidence that will serve you in all social settings.

- **Awkward Algorithm:** Develop a daily routine where you reflect on moments of awkwardness. Whether it's a stumble in conversation or a misstep in social protocol, record the instance and your reaction to it. Consider what triggered the awkward feeling. Was it a mismatch of expectations, a new environment, or perhaps an unfamiliar social cue? Each day, as you note these moments, also write down one thing you learned from them and how you might adapt in the future. This ongoing practice is not just about managing awkwardness; it's about embracing it as a natural part of human interaction and growth, turning moments of discomfort into opportunities for learning and personal development.

- **Mindfulness in Conversation:** Incorporating mindfulness into your conversations is a transformative practice that can deepen connections and enhance understanding. Begin by anchoring yourself in the present moment. Set aside distractions and give your full attention to the person you're speaking with. Listen with the intent to understand, not just to respond. Observe their body language, tone of voice, and facial expressions—these nonverbal cues can often communicate more than words alone.

- Actively engaging in the conversation with curiosity allows for a more authentic exchange. Ask questions, reflect back what you've heard, and pause before replying to ensure that your responses are thoughtful. By practicing mindfulness, you honor both your conversation partner and yourself, fostering a sense of ease and genuine interaction that can lead to more meaningful and rewarding social interactions.

- **Embracing Vulnerability:** Embracing vulnerability is a courageous step towards building authentic connections.

When you allow yourself to be vulnerable, you admit to your discomforts or uncertainties, making it a point of strength rather than weakness. This act can resonate deeply with others, as everyone experiences moments of self-doubt or awkwardness. By sharing your true self, you give permission to others to do the same, fostering a space where genuine interactions can flourish.

Such openness can dissolve barriers, creating a space where people feel seen and understood. Vulnerability, when met with empathy, builds trust and establishes a solid foundation for relationships. It's about showing up as you are, engaging with honesty, and being willing to connect on a deeper level. This shared human experience can change awkward moments into opportunities for deeper connection and mutual support.

As we wrap up Chapter 9, you may now have a renewed perspective on awkwardness, viewing it not as a flaw to be hidden but as an aspect of social interaction to be understood and embraced. This chapter encourages you to see the value in these uncomfortable moments and to use them as stepping stones to building stronger, more authentic relationships. Awkwardness, when approached with curiosity and compassion, can become a gateway to personal development and social harmony.

10

Bordem

oredom, often dismissed as a trivial or negative emotion, actually serves an important purpose in signaling a need for
change or stimulation. In Chapter 10, we look at the roots of boredom, examining how it arises and what it can teach us about our
needs and desires. This chapter offers strategies to not only allevi-
ate boredom but to harness it as a force for personal growth and
engagement with the world around you.

UNDERSTANDING THE ROOTS OF BOREDOM

Boredom can emerge from a variety of sources, including lack
of novelty, insufficient challenge, or a mismatch between our activities and interests. It's a signal from our brain that we are not
finding meaning or purpose in our current situation. We'll explore stories such as Leo's, a retired engineer who initially strug-
gles with the monotony of his days but discovers a latent passion
for gardening that reinvigorates his sense of purpose and connection to the cycle of life.

LEO

In the sleepy town of Seabreeze Haven, Leo's retirement unfolded like an unending Sunday afternoon, long and languid. The retired engineer, once accustomed to the precise rhythm of machinery and the thrill of problem-solving, found himself adrift in a sea of time, each day indistinguishable from the last. The meticulous mind that had once orchestrated the dance of gears and pulleys now only kept the quiet company of ticking clocks and the soft hum of routine.

Leo's house, a shrine to his former life, was peppered with relics of his engineering feats: framed patents, dusty blueprints, and models of structures that stood as monuments to his career. But their silent stillness mirrored the inertia of his current life, a stark contrast to the dynamic world he once shaped.

The shift began subtly, with a single pot of basil on the kitchen windowsill. The sprightly green leaves, so full of zest, caught his attention day after day. He marveled at their growth, a steady, unfurling timeline that stood in contrast to the static displays on his shelves. It wasn't long before the basil was joined by chives, parsley, and a shy mint plant that quivered in the breeze from the open window.

The transformation of his garden—and of Leo himself—blossomed from there. The backyard, previously just a space to be mowed and maintained, became a canvas for his new passion. He approached it with an engineer's mind, researching, planning, and executing with precision, but also with a newfound reverence for the organic unpredictability of nature.

With each seed sown and each plant nurtured, Leo found himself rooting in a new phase of life. The garden, with its cycles of growth and decay, became a living metaphor for his own evolution. He began to understand the quiet wisdom of plants, how they yield to the elements, and yet persist.

His hands, once used to drawing lines and angles, now bore the stains of soil and the scent of thyme. The neighbors started to take notice, first with curious glances, then with questions, and eventually with requests for advice. Leo's garden grew into a community hub, a place of gathering, learning, and sharing.

The boredom that once clouded his days like a relentless fog lifted, revealing a landscape vibrant with the colors of zinnias and the verdant textures of vegetable plots. Leo, the retired engineer, had found a new rhythm to his life, one that pulsed with the quiet yet persistent beat of the earth. His connection to the cycle of life was no longer abstract; it was there, in the tender sprout of a pea plant and the robust red of a ripening tomato.

In Seabreeze Haven, Leo's story is a reminder that even in the stillness of life's later chapters, there is potential for rediscovery—a joy in the simple act of tending to life in all its forms. His journey through the garden's gates shows us that purpose can be found and nurtured, even from the depths of the most monotonous soil.

VISUALIZATION EXERCISES

Visualization Exercise 1: The Canvas of Possibilities

Close your eyes and picture yourself sitting in front of a blank canvas in a tranquil, sunlit room. The canvas represents your day, and it's up to you to create a masterpiece. Visualize yourself picking up a brush dipped in a color that signifies an activity or thought that brings you joy or curiosity. With each stroke, watch as the blank canvas transforms into a vibrant painting, each color and shape representing a new possibility or a rediscovered passion. Feel the satisfaction as the boredom fades away, replaced by the creation of your own design. Allow yourself to be fully immersed in the act of painting your day with activities that energize and inspire you. What does your canvas look like? How do you feel as you bring color and life to what was once empty?

Visualization Exercise 2: The Library of Wonders

Imagine walking into a vast, ancient library. Each book on the countless shelves contains knowledge, stories, and ideas from all over the world and different periods of time. This library is the embodiment of all there is to learn and explore. As you wander through the aisles, let your hand brush against the spines, feeling the texture and sensing the wisdom they hold. Pull a book from the shelf, something that piques your interest. As you open it, visualize the words lifting off the pages and surrounding you, inviting you to dive into a new realm. With each word and image that you absorb, feel the boredom being replaced by fascination and a hunger to learn more. What subjects draw you in? How does it feel to be surrounded by so much potential for discovery?

Visualization Exercise 3: The Journey of the Mind

In your mind's eye, see yourself standing at the beginning of a path that stretches out through an enchanting forest. This path represents your stream of consciousness, winding and ever-changing. Begin to walk, and as you do, notice the thoughts that arise. Instead of pushing away the mundane or the repetitive, acknowledge them and then imagine them as leaves falling onto the path. Keep walking and pay attention to the new thoughts that start to emerge—thoughts of hobbies you've wanted to try, places you wish to visit, or skills you'd like to develop. With each step, let the ideas become more vivid and the path more interesting. Where does it lead you? What new landscapes of the mind do you encounter, and how do they transform the journey from a walk through the forest to an adventure through your own inner world?

ACTIVITIES TO COUNTERACT BOREDOM AND FOSTER ENGAGEMENT

1. **Interest Exploration:** Exploring new interests or rekindling old hobbies can be a refreshing change from the daily grind. It invites a sense of excitement and discovery that can renew your zest for life. To start this process, reflect on activities that once brought you joy or those you've always been curious about. Whether it's painting, hiking, coding, or playing an instrument, set aside dedicated time each week to focus on these passions. Remember, the goal is not to achieve perfection or mastery from the outset but to savor the learning process and the joy it brings. Permit yourself to be a beginner, to make mistakes, and to grow. Experi-

menting with activities outside your norm can open up new perspectives, stimulate creativity, and may even lead to unexpected opportunities. Embrace the adventure of interest exploration as a path to personal enrichment and joy.

2. **Volunteering:** Volunteering is an enriching experience that offers more than just a remedy for boredom. It is a way to connect with your community and make a positive impact on the lives of others. By giving your time and skills to causes you care about, you can find a renewed sense of purpose and meaning in your daily life. Engaging in volunteer work allows you to step outside of yourself and contribute to something larger. It can be incredibly rewarding and fulfilling, providing a sense of accomplishment that routine tasks may not offer. You might try helping at a local food bank, tutoring students, or caring for animals at a shelter; each act of service strengthens community bonds and enriches your own life with new relationships and experiences. Embrace the opportunity to volunteer and discover the joy of making a difference.

3. **Mindful Observation:** Engage in the art of mindful observation by taking a quiet moment to really notice the world around you. This isn't just looking; it's seeing—acknowledging the many colors, textures, and movements that usually fade into the backdrop of your busy days. Start with something small, like the pattern of a leaf or the varied hues in a piece of stone. Consider its place in the larger scene, its role, and its beauty. Let this attention to detail broaden your perspective, helping you appreciate the ordinary as extraordinary. This practice can enhance your observational skills and also foster a deeper connection with your surroundings, encouraging a sense of wonder and curiosity. Over time,

you might find that this mindful approach not only enriches your experiences but also cultivates a greater appreciation for the subtleties of life that previously slipped by unnoticed.

4. **Skill Development:** For those feeling the monotony of routine, consider the dynamic world of skill development to revive your zest for learning. The internet brims with online courses catering to every interest imaginable, from learning a new language to mastering a musical instrument. Local workshops, too, offer a chance to immerse yourself in a hands-on experience, perhaps pottery or gardening, bringing you into a community of like-minded learners. Each lesson completed and every project finished isn't just about gaining a new skill—it's a stepping stone toward personal growth and satisfaction. The act of learning is an achievement in itself, sparking a sense of progress and pride. So dive into that class you've always been curious about and let the journey of continuous learning break the cycle of boredom, leading you to unexpected heights of personal fulfillment.

5. **Boredom Algorithm Daily:** To bypass the still waters of boredom, become attuned to moments when tedium creeps into your day. It may be during mundane tasks or in quiet pauses, but it's within these times that opportunity lies. Spark your curiosity by searching for an intriguing facet in the dreariness around you—anything that can transform the moment with a touch of wonder or a question that leads you further. If the doldrums persist, pivot to an activity that stirs your thoughts or senses; keep an arsenal of engaging diversions close at hand. Let these lulls be the impetus to hone a skill or revisit a beloved hobby, turning idle time into a canvas for creativity and learning. As dusk falls, reflect on your

encounters with boredom: what strategies invigorated your spirit, what attempts fell flat? Use these insights to refine your approach, allowing each day to take you a step closer to mastering the art of turning listlessness into a catalyst for personal enrichment.

By now, you may understand that boredom is not just a void to be filled but an invitation to reconnect with your passions and the vibrant world around you. The activities and insights provided will equip you with the means to transform moments of boredom into opportunities for innovation, learning, and personal enrichment. Boredom, then, becomes not a pitfall of inactivity but a chance for active exploration and self-discovery.

11

Calmness

Calmness is not merely the absence of stress; it is a cultivated state of inner peace and clarity. In Chapter 11, we delve into the pursuit of this tranquil state, exploring how calmness can be an anchor in our bustling lives. This chapter presents methods to cultivate calmness amidst chaos, enabling us to weather life's storms with serenity and strength.

THE QUEST FOR INNER PEACE

The quest for inner peace takes us to the core of our well-being. It's about finding balance in our thoughts and emotions, and maintaining a sense of tranquility regardless of external circumstances. We'll explore the tale of Nora, a paramedic who practices calmness in the eye of life's literal storms, offering her a clarity that enhances her ability to help others.

NORA

In Seabreeze Haven, a town where the lull and roar of the sea mirrored the pulse of life itself, Nora stood as a bastion of serenity. A paramedic whose life was intertwined with the emergencies and urgencies of the townspeople, she was known not just for her skilled hands but also for the tranquil spirit she embodied, even amidst chaos.

Nora's journey into the heart of calmness began early in her career, when the tempest of her first crisis call mirrored the storm that raged outside the ambulance windows. It was then that she discovered the eye of the storm within herself—a place of stillness that allowed her to think with precision and act with compassion.

Over time, her practice of calmness became as much a part of her routine as checking her medical supplies. Before each shift, she would close her eyes and take deep, grounding breaths, envisioning herself at the center of a storm, unaffected by the winds of panic and fear swirling around her. This visualization anchored her, so when the sirens wailed, she was ready, her heartbeat a steady drum in the cacophony.

The people of Seabreeze Haven spoke of Nora's remarkable composure as if it were a healing balm. Patients recalled how her soothing voice had been the lifeline they clung to as they were pulled from the wreckage of accidents or the depths of illness. Her presence was a promise that even in the worst moments, someone was there, unwavering, ready to guide them back to safety.

Nora's gift for calmness transcended her work. She volunteered to teach first-aid classes, imparting her knowledge and her philosophy that the clarity found in calmness was the greatest ally in any emergency. Her students learned not just techniques but also the art of stillness in the face of adversity.

But perhaps where her influence was felt most deeply was at the local high school, where she led stress management workshops for teenagers coping with the storms of adolescence. She gave them tools—a mindfulness meditation, a breathing exercise, a way to find the eye of their own internal storms—to help them manage their young lives.

In Seabreeze Haven, Nora's story is a testament to the power of calm in a world that often feels like a relentless gale. Her legacy is one of lives saved not only by her hands but also by her heart—a heart that beats to the rhythm of the quiet strength that is the core of all she does. She is a reminder that within each of us is an eye of the storm, a center of calmness that can bring clarity and hope, even on the most turbulent of days.

VISUALIZATION EXERCISES

Visualization Exercise 1: The Lake of Tranquility

Find a quiet space where you can relax without interruption. Close your eyes and take a few deep breaths, letting the rhythm of your inhalation and exhalation steady your mind. Now, picture yourself sitting by the edge of a still and peaceful lake. The surface of the water is a perfect mirror, reflecting the serene blue of the sky and the gentle green of the surrounding trees. With each breath you take, imagine any tension or stress you feel dissolving into the lake, leaving you lighter and more at peace. Watch the ripples as they gently move away from you, taking your stress further and further away until the surface is calm once again. Sit with this image for a few moments, enjoying the sense of complete relaxation that envelops you.

Visualization Exercise 2: The Breathing Sphere

Begin by envisioning a glowing sphere in front of you. This sphere represents your breath and your state of calm. As you breathe in, visualize the sphere expanding smoothly, absorbing all your worries and stress. Hold that breath for a moment, letting the sphere shimmer with the captured tension. As you exhale, see the sphere contract, releasing all the negative energy back into the universe as neutral elements. With each cycle of breath, the sphere grows brighter and calmer. Feel your body respond in kind, each muscle relaxing as you sync your breathing with the movement of this calming sphere.

Visualization Exercise 3: The Forest Walk

In your mind, step into a lush, green forest. The canopy above shields you from the chaos of the world, and the path underfoot is soft with moss. As you walk, listen to the soothing sounds of the forest: the rustle of leaves, the distant call of a bird, the whisper of the wind. With each step, imagine drawing in the tranquility of the forest. Feel the calm energy of nature enter your body from the soles of your feet and spread upward. Notice how the forest is alive, yet deeply peaceful, and allow that peaceful energy to infuse your being, replacing any feelings of anxiety or agitation with the forest's timeless serenity.

TECHNIQUES TO CULTIVATE CALM IN CHAOS

1. **Mindfulness Meditation:** Mindfulness meditation offers a serene retreat from the rapid currents of everyday life. It anchors you in the present moment with practices that emphasize the rhythm of your breath and the immediacy of your experiences. As you inhale and exhale deliberately, you'll find your attention drawn away from past regrets and future anxieties, into the here and now. This centered state doesn't just bring tranquility amidst chaos; it enhances your awareness, allowing you to engage more fully with life as it unfolds. Even a few minutes a day can transform a hectic routine into a dance of deliberate action, creating a lasting oasis of peace that rejuvenates the spirit and sharpens the mind.

2. **Nature Retreats:** Nature's embrace is an exquisite remedy for the noise of life's demands. When you step into the embrace of the wilderness, you step out of the world of man-made stress. Engaging in regular retreats into natural spaces can be profoundly soothing. Whether it's the grounding touch of the earth beneath your bare feet or the symphony of a forest, these experiences reconnect you with a simpler rhythm of existence. They remind you of the world's innate beauty and your place within it. Such moments are not just fleeting pauses; they are profound engagements with life, renewing your spirit and bathing your senses in the essence of peace.

3. **Calm Algorithm:** Commit to a daily practice of integrating moments of tranquility into your routine. Begin by designating a time for stillness, perhaps during the morning light or under the evening stars. Utilize this time for deep breath-

ing exercises or a short meditative walk in nature. Track these moments in a journal, noting the serenity they instill. Over time, this algorithm will not only enhance your daily calm but also build a resilient foundation for inner peace, ready to support you amidst life's inevitable turbulence.

4. **Digital Detox:** To find peace in a digital world, consider setting aside specific times each day when you step away from screens. This might be during meals, the first hour after waking, or before bedtime. Use these moments to connect with the tangible world around you—indulge in the aroma of your morning coffee, the texture of the book you're reading, or the soothing practice of deep breathing. This mindful distancing from electronic noise brings serenity to your day and also helps recalibrate your attention to the present, nurturing a more peaceful mindset.

5. **Gratitude Exercises:** Embracing gratitude can transform your perspective. Start a daily journal, writing down three things you're grateful for each day. It could be as simple as a warming sunrise, a kind gesture from a friend, or progress in a personal project. This simple act draws your attention away from life's stressors and toward its gifts, building a sense of contentment and stability. Over time, you'll notice a shift to a more grounded and serene outlook, where appreciation is habitual and peace more readily attained.

You now have a toolkit to help you seek and maintain calmness in both tranquil and trying times. Calmness is a skill that can be developed and a treasure that, once found, can transform the quality of your life. This state is not a distant shoreline but a haven that resides within, accessible with the right techniques and a mindful approach.

12

Confusion

Confusion often feels like wandering through a fog, where the familiar becomes obscured and decision-making seems daunting. In this chapter, we acknowledge confusion not as a weakness but as a natural part of the process of understanding. You'll be guided through the haze of confusion to find clarity and confidence in your decisions.

NAVIGATING THROUGH FOG: DEALING WITH CONFUSION

Confusion can stem from a lack of information, overwhelming options, or internal conflict. It signals a need to pause, reflect, and seek understanding. Through the story of Marcus, a town planner who faces clashing opinions on a new community project, readers will see how embracing confusion can lead to comprehensive solutions that align with communal values.

Marcus

In Seabreeze Haven, a picturesque town where every voice mattered and every opinion held weight, Marcus the town planner found himself at the helm of a complex new community project. The task was to revitalize the old dock area, a place steeped in history but worn by time, and opinions on its future were as varied as the town's vibrant inhabitants.

Marcus, with his keen eye for detail and his methodical mind, had drafted plans that he believed would satisfy the most pressing concerns. However, he quickly discovered that the community's vision for the docks was a mosaic of conflicting desires and dreams. The fishermen sought to preserve the docks' functional heritage, the local businesses pushed for commercial development, and the artists' community imagined a hub that could become the heartbeat of Seabreeze Haven's rich cultural heritage.

The meetings were a cacophony of voices and views, with Marcus at the center, trying to weave a coherent narrative from the discordant strands of conversation. The more he listened, the deeper the fog of confusion seemed to settle upon him. The project, meant to unify, was paradoxically dividing the community he loved.

In the midst of this confusion, Marcus had an epiphany. Instead of shying away from the chaos, he chose to embrace it. He organized a series of town halls, not with the intent to come up with immediate solutions, but to get to the heart of the community's tangled thoughts. He listened, he noted, and most importantly, he understood that confusion was not an obstacle but a path to genuine understanding.

Through these candid discussions, a pattern began to emerge. The seemingly divergent views had a common thread: a love for Seabreeze Haven and a deep-rooted desire to see it thrive. Marcus harnessed this collective passion and guided the community through a process of collaborative design thinking. Each suggestion was a piece of a puzzle, and when considered together, they began to form a picture that honored the town's heritage while embracing progress.

The final plan for the docks was a result of the town's collective imagination. It featured a modern marina that respected the fishermen's needs, spaces for local businesses, and areas dedicated to arts and cultural festivities. The once-confusing array of ideas had coalesced into a project that everyone could take pride in, attesting to the town's unity and Marcus's vision.

In Seabreeze Haven, Marcus's story is a narrative of clarity found within confusion. It's a tale that reminds its residents that even the thickest fog can be navigated with patience and a willingness to embrace the wisdom within the whirlwind of collective thoughts. And for Marcus, it became a professional legacy, proof that the best-laid plans are those that are drawn not with a single hand but with the many hands of a community coming together.

VISUALIZATION EXERCISES

Visualization Exercise 1: The Mosaic of Thoughts

Sit comfortably and close your eyes. Begin by picturing yourself in a room with walls covered in blank tiles, each tile representing a thought or idea. As you consider a decision or problem causing you confusion, visualize each aspect of it appearing on a tile. At first, the tiles may seem to be randomly placed, creating a disjointed mosaic. Now, imagine stepping back and looking at the tiles from a distance. Gradually, start rearranging them, finding connections and patterns until a clear image or solution emerges. Breathe deeply as clarity takes shape, feeling the confusion dissipate as you form a complete, coherent picture. Take a moment to appreciate the order you've created from the chaos.

Visualization Exercise 2: The Foggy Path

Inhale deeply and imagine yourself standing at the start of a foggy forest path. The thick mist represents the confusion you feel. With each step forward on the path, take a deep breath, and as you exhale, picture the fog clearing slightly. With each breath and step, the path becomes more visible, and your direction becomes clearer. The uncertainty and confusion are slowly lifting, replaced by an increasing sense of direction and purpose. Continue walking until the path is completely clear, and you're bathed in the warm, reassuring light at the forest's edge.

Visualization Exercise 3: Untangling the Knots

Imagine yourself sitting in a peaceful garden, surrounded by colorful flowers and gentle breezes. In your hands, you hold a ball of tangled yarn, representing the confusion you feel. Take a deep breath, and as you exhale, visualize yourself slowly and patiently untangling the knots. With each gentle movement, the yarn begins to loosen and unravel, revealing a long, smooth strand. As the yarn untangles, feel your mind becoming clearer and more organized. With each knot that you release, experience a sense of relief and clarity, as if your thoughts are aligning and becoming more coherent. When the yarn is completely untangled, imagine wrapping it neatly into a perfect ball, feeling a sense of accomplishment and clarity. When you're ready, open your eyes, bringing this sense of clarity and calm into the present moment..

TOOLS FOR CLARITY AND DECISION-MAKING

1. **Mind Mapping:** Mind mapping is a dynamic and visual method to organize your thoughts, especially when you're faced with confusion. Imagine your central problem or question at the center, and from there, branch out to all the related aspects, concerns, or tasks. This not only helps in structuring your thoughts but also in identifying connections and priorities. By creating a mind map, you give yourself a bird's-eye view of complex situations, facilitating a pathway through the maze of confusion to the clarity of well-considered decisions. It's a step towards transforming tangled thoughts into a roadmap for action.

2. **Pro-Con Lists:** Pro-con lists are a timeless strategy for making sense of difficult choices. By simply drawing a line down the middle of a page, labeling one side "Pros" and the other "Cons", you give structure to the debate swirling in your mind. List all the positive outcomes and advantages on one side and the potential drawbacks and negative consequences on the other. This process can help you crystallize your thoughts, weigh different aspects of a decision, and lead you to a conclusion that balances benefits against costs. It's an exercise in critical thinking that can bring you closer to a decision you can stand by confidently.

3. **Focused Rest:** Taking intentional breaks for focused rest can be incredibly beneficial, especially when you're feeling overwhelmed by confusion. Engage in a brief walk or a few moments of meditation to give your brain a chance to unwind and sort through thoughts and information away from the conscious effort. These pauses in your day allow your subconscious to work through complex issues, offering clarity when you return to the task at hand. This isn't idle time. It's an investment in more effective problem-solving and a calmer mental state.

4. **Seeking Diverse Perspectives:** Consulting with others to hear diverse viewpoints is a strategy that can significantly help when you're confronted with confusion. This approach can shed new light on a situation, offering insights you might not have considered on your own. Whether it's through structured brainstorming sessions, casual conversations, or seeking out opinions from different cultural or professional backgrounds, embracing a range of perspectives can guide you to innovative solutions and clearer understanding. Remember, what might be a blind spot for you could be clear to someone with a different set of experiences.

5. **Confusion Algorithm:** Make it a daily habit to reflect on the moments when you feel uncertain or conflicted. Note the situation, your initial thoughts, and how you choose to seek clarity. You can try conversations with others, time for focused rest, or employing decision-making tools like mind mapping, then track the effectiveness of these strategies over time. This reflective practice can gradually guide you in developing personalized methods for mitigating confusion and enhancing your decision-making skills.

As the chapter concludes, reflect on your new understanding of confusion as an integral part of the learning and growth process. The tools and strategies provided will equip you to cut through the fog of confusion, enabling you to make informed and deliberate decisions. Confusion is just a temporary state on the road to clear understanding and wise choices.

13

Craving

Cravings are intense desires that pull us toward something with an almost magnetic force, whether it's a person, an experience, or a chocolate bar. In Chapter 13, we explore the intricate nature of desire and craving and the ways they drive us. We also look at how to balance these strong desires with a mindful approach to living, ensuring our cravings lead us to fulfillment rather than away from it.

THE NATURE OF DESIRE AND CRAVING

Desire is a fundamental human experience, rooted in our biology and psychology. It can motivate us to pursue goals and meet our needs. Craving takes this one step further, embodying a powerful yearning for immediate satisfaction. This section of the chapter will consider how cravings can both positively motivate us and sometimes lead us astray. We'll introduce readers to Amelia, a chef whose craving for culinary perfection fuels her career but also blinds her to life's simpler pleasures until she learns to find balance.

AMELIA

Amelia's culinary journey in Seabreeze Haven was a driven pursuit of gastronomic excellence. As the head chef of the renowned Azure Tide restaurant, her days were a whirlwind of sizzling pans and orchestral commands, her every waking hour dedicated to the art that danced upon the palates of her patrons.

Her dedication to her craft was legendary; her kitchen, a temple where the freshest local ingredients were transformed into masterpieces of flavor and presentation. Yet in her relentless search for the perfect dish, the quintessential flavor, the precise garnish, Amelia's life outside the stainless-steel confines of her kitchen had simmered down to a mere whisper.

The irony was not lost on her. A creator of delightful meals, she often missed the joy found in the simplicity of a ripe, sun-warmed peach or the rustic charm of a freshly baked loaf of bread. Her world was filled with exotic spices and avant-garde techniques, but the simple act of breaking bread with old friends, the laughter shared over a pot of stew, had become unfamiliar to her.

The epiphany came on a quiet Monday, her rare day off, when Amelia found herself walking the windswept beach of Seabreeze Haven. There, she stumbled upon a small picnic where a group of locals invited her to join their humble feast. Hesitant at first, she soon found herself enveloped in the warmth of uncomplicated camaraderie, the kind that flourished over shared sandwiches and hand-picked berries.

As the salt-laden breeze mingled with the laughter of her new-found companions, Amelia realized that her craving for culinary perfection had overshadowed the fundamental joy of cooking—the connection it fostered, the memories it seasoned, and the simple pleasure it could bring. She discovered a new craving, not for perfection, but for the balance that honored both her exceptional talent and the basic human need for connection and joy.

Inspired by this revelation, Amelia began to infuse her approach to cooking with this newfound philosophy. She hosted community dinners at Azure Tide, where sophisticated cuisine met the comforting embrace of home-cooked meals. She volunteered to teach cooking classes, sharing not only her knowledge but also her appreciation for the simple act of preparing food together.

In the end, Amelia's story is a celebration of balance—a life where the pursuit of excellence coexists with the appreciation of life's simple pleasures. Her journey taught her that sometimes, the most profound cravings are not only those of the palate but also of the heart. And in Seabreeze Haven, she found that balance, along with a deeper understanding of the true essence of her craft and the gifts it could bring to both herself and her community.

VISUALIZATION EXERCISES

Visualization Exercise 1: The Orchard of Delights

Imagine yourself wandering through a lush orchard, filled with the ripest and most succulent fruits. Each tree represents a different craving you have—for food, for accomplishment, for connection. As you walk, take time to acknowledge each craving by picking a piece of fruit from the tree. Examine it, smell it, and taste it, savoring the flavors and the fulfillment it brings. Consider how satisfying this craving can nourish other parts of your life. With each fruit you savor, visualize how you can satisfy these desires in a balanced way that contributes to your overall well-being.

Visualization Exercise 2: The Banquet of Balance

Close your eyes and picture a grand banquet table before you, laden with an array of dishes, each embodying a different aspect of your life where you feel a strong craving. There are dishes that represent professional success, personal relationships, health, and personal growth. Visualize yourself sampling from each dish, appreciating the unique flavors and experiences they bring. Reflect on how indulging in each aspect in moderation can lead to a more balanced life. Feel the sense of contentment and fullness that comes not from overindulgence in one area, but from enjoying a little of each.

Visualization Exercise 3: The River of Desires

See yourself standing by a gently flowing river. This river symbolizes your stream of desires and cravings. Notice how some currents run strong and fast, while others are slower, each representing the intensity of different cravings. Visualize yourself dipping a container into the river, drawing out some of the water. This water is the energy and time you'll devote to your cravings. Pour some into several small channels leading off the river, creating pathways that allow you to address each craving without the main current becoming overwhelming or destructive. Feel a sense of control and intentionality as you manage the flow, directing it to nourish your life in a balanced and sustainable way.

BALANCING CRAVINGS AND MINDFUL LIVING

1. **Identifying Underlying Needs:** Identifying the roots of our cravings can be an enlightening experience. Cravings often hint at deeper needs that we might not be consciously aware of. To uncover these underlying needs, you can begin by monitoring your cravings as they arise. Keep a journal to note when a craving hits, what it is directed toward, and what emotions or situations trigger it. By observing patterns over time, you may discover that cravings are not random but linked to specific emotional states, unmet needs, or even habitual responses. Regularly taking time to sit quietly and reflect can also provide insights. Ask yourself what you're really seeking in moments of craving. Is it comfort, excitement, a sense of belonging, or perhaps an escape from boredom or stress? As you learn more about your cravings' true origins, you'll be better equipped to satisfy them in healthy and fulfilling ways.

2. **Mindful Consumption:** Mindful consumption is a practice that can transform the way we respond to our cravings. By adopting mindfulness, you can create a pause between the urge to satisfy a craving and the action you take. In these moments of pause, give yourself space to breathe deeply and acknowledge the craving without judgment. Ask yourself: Is this craving a response to an emotional need? What will be the consequences of indulging in it? Will it serve my well-being in the long run? This isn't about suppressing desires, but rather understanding them and making choices

that align with your deeper values and long-term goals. This mindfulness can lead to a more balanced life where immediate gratifications are weighed against their future impact on your health, happiness, and overall life satisfaction.

3. **Cultivating Alternative Fulfillments:** Exploring personal interests and contributing to the community can offer a deep sense of satisfaction that goes beyond the temporary. Consider taking up hobbies that challenge your intellect or creativity; they can become a source of pride and joy, contributing to your identity and skills. Engaging in community service connects you with others, making you an active participant in shaping a better world. Such activities are not only fulfilling but also help in building a legacy that reflects your values and passions. This sense of alignment with your long-term well-being can be incredibly rewarding and a wellspring for continued personal growth.

4. **Setting Intentions:** Intention-setting can transform how we approach our desires, focusing our attention and energies on what truly matters. By clearly defining our aspirations, we create a roadmap for our actions and decisions. This mindful approach allows us to discern and prioritize desires that align with our core values, leading to more meaningful and satisfying experiences. Setting intentions is a proactive step toward a fulfilling life, one where each choice is deliberate, and each action is infused with purpose. It's about inviting into our life what resonates with our authentic self, creating a life rich in intention.

5. **Reflection:** Reflecting on the cycles of our cravings is a powerful way to uncover the patterns that drive our actions. By integrating reflective practices into your routine, you begin to notice the ebbs and flows of desire and how they can

lead to habitual responses. Consider setting aside time each day for introspection, perhaps through journaling or quiet contemplation, to observe these patterns without judgment. Recognize the triggers, the thoughts that spin from these cravings, and the behaviors they invoke. With this awareness, you can start to discern whether these cycles serve you well or if they're holding you back, empowering you to make choices that reflect your deeper goals and values. This is the crux of the reflection, transforming self-understanding into actionable change.

You've hopefully begun to understand the complex interplay between craving, desire, and mindful living. You now have practical tools to manage cravings in a healthy way, aligning your desires with your overall goals for well-being. Cravings, once understood and balanced, can become a source of joy rather than a pitfall, contributing to a rich and satisfying life.

14

Disgust

Disgust, a powerful emotional response that protects us from harm, can have a significant impact on our behavior and interactions. This visceral reaction can range from mild distaste to intense revulsion. In the following chapter, we dissect the emotion of disgust to understand its origins and the ways it influences our lives. We also explore strategies for managing and responding to stimuli that disgusts in a healthy and constructive manner.

DISSECTING DISGUST: ORIGINS AND IMPACTS

The origins of disgust are rooted in evolution, serving as a defense mechanism against potential contaminants and dangers. This emotional response can be triggered by various stimuli, including certain foods, behaviors, or ethical violations. We will investigate disgust's evolutionary purpose and how this primal reaction has expanded into the social and moral domains. You will be introduced to cases like that of Sarah, a healthcare worker who confronts her initial feelings of disgust to provide compassionate care, and David, whose aversion to dishonesty drives his commitment to integrity in his business dealings.

SARAH

In the bustling corridors of Seabreeze Haven's local hospital, Sarah moved with a sense of purpose that only a life dedicated to the healing arts can bestow. As a healthcare worker, her days were a study of human fragility and resilience, her hands instruments of the care she provided.

Despite her unwavering commitment, Sarah faced a challenge not uncommon in her field: the visceral reaction of disgust that certain medical situations evoked. It was a natural, human response, yet it stood in stark contrast to the empathy that beat at the heart of her vocation.

The confrontation with her instinctual revulsion came one rain-drenched morning when an emergency brought a patient in dire need, his condition testing the boundaries of Sarah's professional detachment. The sight and smell that greeted her as the ambulance doors swung open were a stark affront to the senses, a harsh reminder of the more gruesome aspects of her calling.

Yet, within Sarah, there existed a wellspring of compassion deeper than any momentary feeling of disgust. As she donned her gloves and focused on the person in need before her, her initial recoil was replaced by the recognition of her role as a healer. The vulnerability of the human condition, in all its forms, was laid bare before her, and with it, the honor of being able to offer comfort and aid.

In the days that followed, Sarah reflected on the experience, seeking a path through the tangled underbrush of her reactions.

She turned to her mentors, seasoned professionals who had navigated their own journeys through the emotional landscape of healthcare. Their wisdom, coupled with Sarah's introspection, led her to a transformative realization: disgust, though natural, could be acknowledged and then set aside for the sake of greater good.

Sarah began to share her realization with new colleagues, guiding them through the emotional complexities of their noble profession. Together, they explored the balance between maintaining a clinical perspective and embracing the deeply human touch essential to their work.

Sarah's story, unfolding within the wards and rooms of the hospital, illustrates the triumph of empathy over aversion, of professionalism over personal discomfort. It is a reminder that even the most instinctual human responses can be overcome by the strength of our higher callings.

In the heart of Seabreeze Haven, Sarah's tale is spoken of with respect—a narrative of a caregiver who, through confronting her own challenges, found a way to provide not just medical interventions but truly compassionate care.

DAVID

In Seabreeze Haven, a town that prided itself on the honest toil of its people and the clear skies above, David was known as much for his business acumen as for his unyielding integrity. As the owner of a local construction company, he had built more than homes and offices; he had built a reputation as a man who stood by his word, his handshake as solid as the foundations he poured.

David's path had not always been paved with certainty. Early in his career, he had witnessed the corrosive nature of dishonesty in business, seeing firsthand how cut corners and untruths could erode trust like salt air on untreated wood. This exposure to the underbelly of his trade filled him with a deep sense of disgust that became the bedrock upon which he established his own company.

The disgust that David felt toward dishonesty went beyond mere distaste. It was a visceral response that guided his decisions and shaped the culture of his business. He was meticulous in his transparency, ensuring that clients knew exactly what to expect, from the initial blueprint to the final brick. His contracts were clear, his timelines realistic, his pricing fair.

In meetings, David's forthright manner sometimes came across as brusque, his disdain for industry double-talk evident in his curt nods and the set line of his jaw. But those who worked with him knew that his directness was a shield against the miscommunications and deceptions that plagued the field.

His employees, a loyal crew who mirrored his values, became advocates for integrity in an industry often clouded by skepticism. They knew that their leader's aversion to dishonesty meant that their labor was respected, their efforts recognized, and their own reputations unblemished by association.

David's commitment to integrity extended beyond the job site. He conducted workshops for young entrepreneurs, teaching them that long-term success was measured not in profit margins alone but in the trust one built along the way. His lessons, rooted in personal anecdotes that laid bare the ugliness of deceit, inspired a new generation to hold fast to their principles.

In Seabreeze Haven, David's story became a parable of professional honor. He showed that disgust, a powerful emotional response, could be channeled into a force for good, steering a course through the sometimes-murky waters of business with a compass set firmly on integrity. His legacy was not just in the structures that stood tall against the Haven's skyline but in the knowledge that they were built on the solid ground of honesty and respect.

VISUALIZATION EXERCISES

Visualization Exercise 1: The Cleansing Waterfall

Sit comfortably and take a deep breath. Close your eyes and visualize yourself standing in front of a majestic waterfall in a beautiful, pristine forest. The waterfall represents purity and truth. As you step under the waterfall, imagine it washing away any feelings of disgust, particularly those related to dishonesty or moral discomfort. Feel the cool water as it cascades over you, cleansing you of these negative sensations and replacing them with a sense of clarity and integrity. Notice how your body and mind feel lighter and refreshed as you step out, free from the burden of negative feelings.

Visualization Exercise 2: The Garden of Values

In this visualization, see yourself walking through a vibrant garden where each plant represents one of your core values, such as honesty, transparency, and fairness. Notice a plant that has become overgrown or is wilting—the embodiment of your disgust toward dishonest actions. Approach this plant and carefully prune it, removing the parts that no longer serve the health of your garden. As you do this, reaffirm your commitment to nurturing the positive values that you want to grow and flourish in your life. With each snip, feel your dedication to these values strengthening.

Visualization Exercise 3: The Mirror

Picture yourself standing in front of a mirror that reflects not just your physical appearance but your inner moral landscape. In the reflection, identify any spots or blemishes that symbolize instances where you've felt disgust. Acknowledge these feelings without judgment, understanding they are part of being human. Then, visualize a gentle light radiating from your heart, illuminating these spots and transforming them into lessons that reinforce your commitment to living with integrity. Watch as the mirror reflects a clearer, truer image of who you are and who you strive to be.

HEALTHY APPROACHES TO STIMULI THAT DISGUSTS

Disgust can be a complex and intense emotion that often requires nuanced approaches to understand and manage. Here's how you might handle it:

1. **Cognitive Reframing:** Disgust often arises in response to a stimulus that's perceived as offensive or contaminating. By reframing, you can change your perception of these stimuli. This doesn't mean ignoring your initial reaction, but

rather contextualizing it. Ask yourself why the reaction is happening and consider the rationality of this response. Is the disgust warranted, or is it a learned behavior that can be unlearned?

2. **Exposure Therapy Techniques:** This therapeutic approach can be effective for reducing the intensity of disgust, especially in cases of phobias. It involves gradually and repeatedly exposing yourself to the disgusting stimulus in a controlled and safe environment, thereby decreasing the sensitivity over time. It's a process that requires patience and can often benefit from professional guidance.

3. **Ethical Deliberation:** Disgust can sometimes be an emotional reaction to moral wrongdoing. By engaging in ethical deliberation, you can discern whether your feelings of disgust are informing your moral compass or if they're hindering a deeper understanding of a situation. Reflect on the reasons behind your disgust and challenge yourself to consider different perspectives.

4. **Disgust Algorithm Reflection:** Reflect on the role disgust plays in your life. How do you react to it? Does it serve a protective function, or does it lead to avoidance that holds you back? Understanding your patterns can help you decide if you need to embrace disgust or work towards changing your reactions to it.

5. **Emotional Regulation:** Physical strategies like deep breathing or grounding exercises can help manage the bodily sensations that accompany disgust. These techniques focus on calming the nervous system, allowing you to regain control and reduce the immediate intensity of the emotion. Practice these regularly to become more adept at handling disgust's physical component.

By exploring each of these avenues, you can cultivate a healthier relationship with the feeling of disgust and harness its potential for positive personal growth.

As we close of Chapter 14, you are beginning to build a nuanced understanding of disgust and its place in the human emotional repertoire. With the tools and strategies provided, you are now more prepared to approach disgusting stimuli with a balanced perspective, using your emotional responses as information rather than directives. This chapter empowers you to handle disgust with grace and poise, turning an often-unpleasant feeling into an opportunity for growth and ethical reflection.

15

Empathic Pain

E mpathy allows us to feel the emotional states of others, often leading to a deep sense of compassion and connection. However, when this emotional resonance results in personal distress, it can become empathic pain—a double-edged sword that can be both enlightening and exhausting. This chapter will reveal the complex nature of empathic pain and how to deal with its challenges while maintaining compassion and developing resilience.

THE DOUBLE-EDGED SWORD OF EMPATHY

Empathy enriches our relationships and drives acts of kindness. But absorbing the pain of others can take a toll on our own emotional well-being. In this chapter, we explore how empathic pain can manifest in various scenarios, such as for healthcare professionals, caregivers, or anyone deeply affected by the suffering of others. Through the story of Julian, a social worker who experiences secondary traumatic stress, and Clare who finds herself overwhelmed by global news, we'll examine the impact of empathic pain and strategies to manage it.

Julian and Clare

In the compassionate yet wearied heart of Seabreeze Haven, Julian and Clare lived parallel lives marked by an empathy that often felt like a burden as heavy as the ocean is deep. Julian, a social worker, spent his days navigating the choppy waters of human suffering, absorbing the emotional tumult of those he sought to help. Each case left an imprint on his soul, a residual ache from bearing witness to so much pain.

Clare, on the other hand, found herself drowning in a sea of global turmoil. The daily tide of news stories washed over her, tales of tragedy and injustice from distant lands that left her feeling powerless and heartbroken. Though miles and oceans apart from these events, she felt the weight of the world's sorrows as if they were her own.

Their journeys through the fog of empathic pain began to converge when they both sought refuge in a local support group for those overwhelmed by the emotional toll of caring too much. Julian discovered that his drive to assist those in need had become an all-consuming force, leaving him with secondary traumatic stress that mirrored the trauma of those he helped.

Clare learned that her global awareness, though born from a place of caring, had spiraled into an empathy overload, leaving her paralyzed by the breadth of suffering she felt so deeply.

In this circle of shared experience, Julian and Clare and others like them, found solace and understanding. They spoke of the exhaustion that comes not from the body but from the soul, of the guilt that accompanies the need to step back and of the fear that their empathy might somehow run dry.

Together, they began to devise strategies to manage their empathic pain. Julian adopted routines of self-care, setting boundaries that allowed him to be present for his clients without absorbing their traumas. He learned to leave the stories of the day at the office door, creating a sanctuary at home where peace could thrive.

Clare engaged in a digital detox, limiting her exposure to the relentless stream of news and instead channeled her concern into local action. She volunteered for causes that resonated with her, finding that affecting change, even on a small scale, provided a balm for her empathic wounds.

Their story is a chronicle of hope for those who feel too deeply, a reminder that empathic pain need not be an occupational hazard nor a byproduct of a caring heart. Julian and Clare, along with others in their support group, emerged not with hardened hearts but with reinforced spirits, ready to continue their empathic journeys with renewed resilience and the wisdom that even the deepest care must be tempered with self-compassion.

VISUALIZATION EXERCISES

Visualization Exercise 1: The Shield of Light

Begin by sitting in a quiet, comfortable space. Close your eyes and take several deep breaths, feeling your body relax with each exhale. Now, imagine a gentle, radiant light emanating from your heart center, growing brighter and warmer with each breath. This light represents your compassion and empathy. Visualize it expanding to form a protective shield around you, a barrier that allows you to feel and understand others' pain without it piercing through to harm you. See yourself moving through your day with this shield intact, interacting with those around you, offering support and understanding, while also maintaining your emotional well-being. Remind yourself that you can be a source of comfort without taking on others' pain as your own.

Visualization Exercise 2: The River of Release

Picture yourself sitting by a serene river in a beautiful natural setting. This river flows steadily, representing the stream of empathic connections you experience. Imagine each instance of empathic pain as a leaf falling onto the water's surface. Observe as the river carries these leaves away from you, acknowledging the pain as it flows by but not allowing it to settle within you. With each leaf that drifts down the river, feel your burden of empathic pain lessen, allowing the soothing sounds and sights of the river to bring peace to your soul.

Visualization Exercise 3: The Grounding Tree

See yourself as a strong, deeply rooted tree. Your roots anchor you firmly to the earth, giving you strength and stability. Imagine the empathic pain you feel as a gust of wind rustling through your branches. While you can sway with the wind, acknowledging its presence, your strong roots prevent you from being uprooted. Breathe in the strength from the earth and exhale the pain into the wind. With each breath, feel more grounded and secure, knowing that you can weather the storm of emotions without losing yourself.

BUILDING RESILIENCE AND COMPASSIONATE BOUNDARIES

1. **Self-Care Regimens:** Prioritize activities that nurture your well-being. Engage in regular exercise, find solace in hobbies that light up your spirit, or retreat to nature to rejuvenate. These practices not only restore energy but also provide a healing counterbalance to the emotional toll of empathy.

2. **Emotional Decompression Techniques:** Empathic pain can accumulate, leading to stress. Techniques like journaling offer a way to unpack these emotions, meditation can provide a mental break, and creative outlets like art can transform pain into expression. Each acts as a release valve, allowing you to process and relieve the stress in a healthy way.

3. **Boundary Setting:** It's essential to know where your emotional territory begins and ends. Learn to recognize when to draw the line, saying "no" when necessary, and give yourself permission to step back. Setting healthy boundaries isn't selfish; it's a self-respect that ensures you can continue to be compassionate without losing yourself.

4. **Support Systems:** You don't have to carry the weight of empathic pain alone. Cultivate a network of friends, family, or colleagues who understand and respect your emotional experiences. And remember, seeking professional counseling is a sign of strength, providing a support structure to cope with empathic challenges.

5. **Empathic Pain Algorithm Reflection:** Reflect on the patterns of your empathic pain. When do you feel it most? How does it affect your behavior? Understanding these patterns can inform strategies to manage your empathic responses, turning what might seem like a burden into a source of human connection and compassion.

As this chapter concludes, you have opened insight into the delicate balance of empathic engagement. Empathic pain, while a testament to your humanity, need not be an insurmountable obstacle. With the right tools and knowledge, it is possible to cultivate a compassionate yet resilient approach to empathy, one that honors your connections with others while preserving your own emotional health.

16

Entrancement

Entrancement, a state of being so wholly absorbed or captivated by something that it feels like time stands still, can be a source of deep joy and wonder. In Chapter 16, we delve into the enchanting experience of entrancement, exploring how it can heighten our appreciation for life's marvels and provide a sense of connection to the present moment.

The Enchantment of Entrancement

This captivating emotion can be elicited by a wide array of experiences, from the arts to natural wonders, and even by the flow of work or conversation. We'll discover how entrancement can act as a portal to deeper understanding and enjoyment. For example, readers will meet Lucas, an amateur astronomer whose first glimpse of the night sky through a telescope becomes a transformative experience, igniting a lifelong passion for the cosmos. There's also Eva, a dancer who loses herself in the music and movement, finding a freedom and expression that transcends the ordinary.

LUCAS

In the tranquil coastal enclave of Seabreeze Haven, beneath the grand tapestry of the night sky, there dwelled an amateur astronomer named Lucas. His life, marked by routine and the daily grind, took an extraordinary turn one fateful evening with a serendipitous encounter with a telescope.

The telescope, a relic left to him by an eccentric uncle, was an aperture to the unknown, a portal to the vast cosmos that lay beyond the confines of earthly existence. Lucas, driven by curiosity, set it up in his modest backyard, not realizing that his first gaze through the lens would mark the beginning of a lifelong adventure.

As the dome of heaven came into focus, the celestial bodies hung before him like jewels on the black velvet of space. The craters of the moon, the swirling storms of Jupiter, and the majestic rings of Saturn were no longer just concepts in a textbook but tangible realities, nearly within reach. This singular moment of revelation was not just about the vision of the cosmos but the feeling it evoked—an entrancement that gripped his soul.

The stars whispered ancient secrets, and in their silent murmuring, Lucas found a calling that would consume his nights thereafter. His telescope became his compass, guiding him through the celestial currents. Each observation, each celestial event, from the delicate dance of a meteor shower to the solemn procession of a comet, deepened his enthrallment.

Lucas's newfound passion did not go unnoticed. His enthusiasm spilled over into the community of Seabreeze Haven, where he began to share his nightly vigils with curious neighbors. Together, they would marvel at the wonders above, their collective awe forging bonds of friendship and understanding.

His backyard observatory became a sanctuary not only for him but for many in the town, a place where the worries of the world fell away in favor of the cosmic spectacle. Lucas, once an amateur astronomer in solitude, became the maestro of a symphony of stargazers, his home a place where the community could gather to share in the entrancement of the cosmos.

Lucas's transformation from a layperson to an impassioned astronomer serves to illustrate the power of entrancement. It shows us how a single moment of engagement with beauty can alter the course of a life, turning an ordinary existence into one of perpetual wonder and discovery. In Seabreeze Haven, his story shines as brightly as the stars that inspired it, reminding all who hear it that the universe is not just a space to be studied, but an experience to be cherished.

EVA

In the quaint town of Seabreeze Haven, where the rhythm of the sea's waves set a natural cadence for life, a local dancer named Eva moved to a melody that seemed to echo from the very depths of her being. To the townsfolk, Eva was a figure of grace and poise, her dance studio by the coast a lighthouse of creativity and expression.

From a young age, Eva had found solace in the world of dance, where the strains of music met the flow of motion, creating a language that spoke more expressively than words ever could. In her studio, with its wide windows framing the ocean, she would let the music envelop her.

The dance floor was her canvas, her body the brush, and as she danced, she would lose herself in the choreography of spontaneity and structure. The walls of the studio would dissolve, the floor would give way to open sky, and Eva would find herself in a state of entrancement, her movements a tribute to the beauty of uninhibited expression.

This was where Eva found freedom, her limbs tracing the arcs of her innermost emotions and thoughts. Each performance was an act of vulnerability and strength, an outpouring of her spirit that left the audience spellbound. The purity of her dance was such that to watch Eva was to be pulled into the current of her passion, to be momentarily untethered from the ordinary and swept up into the sublime.

Word of Eva's mesmerizing performances spread beyond the borders of Seabreeze Haven, drawing visitors who longed to experience the enchantment they had heard whispered on the winds. Yet despite her growing acclaim, Eva remained grounded, her soul as barefoot and free as it had been when she first stepped onto the dance floor.

Her entrancement with dance became an example for others who sought liberation from the confines of their own lives. Eva opened her studio to the community, teaching them not just steps and sequences but how to find their own rhythm, their own unique dance with life.

Eva's story is not just one of talent and technique; it is a tale of transcendence. In the town of Seabreeze Haven, she is a reminder of the transformative power of art, and how losing oneself in a passion can lead to discovering a greater sense of self, a symphony of movement and music that resonates with the pulse of the universe itself.

VISUALIZATION EXERCISES

Visualization Exercise 1: The Dance of the Elements

Sit down in a quiet place, close your eyes, and breathe deeply. Let each breath draw you further inward. Visualize yourself standing in a space where the elements of nature surround you—earth under your feet, air swirling around you, water flowing nearby, and a warm fire flickering in the distance. Begin to move your body in response to these elements, slowly at first, then with growing confidence and fluidity. Feel yourself becoming one with the rhythms of nature, losing all sense of time and place as you dance. With each movement, let go of any lingering thoughts, allowing the dance to carry you into a state of pure entrancement. What do you feel as you become one with the dance?

Visualization Exercise 2: The Symphony of Light

Imagine yourself in a darkened room with a single beam of light cutting through the shadows. As you focus on the light, notice how it starts to pulse in time with your heartbeat. In this visualization, allow the light to grow and envelop you, its rhythm guiding you into a trance. The light begins to shift in colors and patterns, each change in the spectrum inviting a new wave of emotion and memory. Surrender to the experience, letting the symphony of light lead you on a journey of sensory and emotional discovery. How do the changing lights influence your state of mind and feeling?

Visualization Exercise 3: The Echo of Silence

Find a comfortable seated position and turn your attention to the silence around you. As you concentrate on the stillness, start to tune into the echo of your own heartbeat, the sound of your breath, the whisper of your presence. Let these subtle sounds expand in your mind, filling the silence with their gentle rhythm. Envision this internal symphony growing louder, resonating with the core of who you are, until everything else falls away, and you're left in a state of focus and absorption. This echo of silence becomes your guide into a deep trance where your sense of self is both heightened and at peace. What insights do you find in this space where only your essence exists?

RECOGNIZING AND APPRECIATING MOMENTS OF CAPTIVATION

1. **Mindful Engagement:** Delve deeply into your passions with full presence. Whether it's getting lost in the melodies of your favorite music, expressing creativity through art, or soaking in the serenity of nature, do it with mindfulness. This intentional presence can elevate the sense of being completely absorbed and enchanted by the moment.

2. **Flow State Activities:** The state of "flow" is where engagement becomes effortless and time seems to stand still. Seek activities that challenge your skills just enough to maintain a captivating balance, like writing that flows from you, competitive gaming that focuses your strategy, engaging sports, or challenging puzzles. These activities facilitate a match between your abilities and the task at hand, leading to entrancing experiences.

3. **Sensory Attunement Practices:** Sharpen your sensory awareness to enrich your perception. Practices like mindful eating, where you savor every flavor and texture, or sensory walks, where you attentively observe your surroundings, can heighten everyday experiences, making them more enthralling.

4. **Entrancement Algorithm Reflection:** Reflect on the experiences that captivate you. What activities lead you to lose track of time? Observing and noting these can help you understand the triggers for your personal states of entrancement and seek them out more deliberately.

5. **Gratitude for the Transcendent:** Recognize and appreciate those moments when you're swept away by the beauty or intensity of an experience. Gratitude for these transcendent moments not only acknowledges their value but can also set the stage for their increased occurrence, deepening your capacity for awe and wonder.

As this chapter comes to a close, you are beginning to develop an appreciation for the power of entrancement and its ability to enrich your life. Recognize opportunities for entrancement in the ordinary, infusing wonderment into your daily life. Entrancement, with its enchanting grip, is shown to be not an escape from reality but a deeper dive into the essence of our existence.

17

Excitment

Excitement is the spark that ignites passion, fuels anticipation, and brings vibrancy to life. In the following chapter, we embrace the thrill of excitement, exploring how it propels us forward and can be channeled into positive outcomes. This chapter encourages readers to understand and seek out excitement in healthy ways, and to use this powerful emotion to enhance their enthusiasm for life and their interests.

THE THRILL OF EXCITEMENT AND ITS PURSUIT

Excitement can serve as a motivator, driving us to explore, innovate, and engage with life more fully. It's a rush of energy that can make us feel alive and eager to take on new challenges. Through stories such as that of Marco, an inventor whose excitement over a new project fuels long hours of dedication and ultimately leads to a groundbreaking discovery, readers will see how excitement can be a force for positive change and achievement.

MARCO

In the vibrant town of Seabreeze Haven, where the spirit of innovation was as constant as the steady lighthouse beam, there lived an inventor named Marco. His workshop, nestled on the edge of town, was a cavern of wonders, filled with half-assembled creations and blueprints that covered the walls like modern frescoes.

Marco's latest venture was born from a moment of pure excitement, a spark ignited by an accidental discovery during one of his many experiments. This new project, he believed, had the potential to revolutionize renewable energy—a wind turbine that could harness the gentlest of breezes with unparalleled efficiency.

The excitement of this discovery consumed him. It became the pulse of his existence, each beat driving him to push beyond the boundaries of the day's hours. Night after night, Marco toiled, his mind racing faster than the hands of the clock, his heart fueled by the exhilaration of potential that lay within his grasp.

His friends and family watched with a blend of concern and admiration as Marco poured his very soul into the project. They worried for his health, for the life he was missing beyond the cluttered confines of his workshop. But they could not deny the brilliance of his vision, nor the infectious nature of his enthusiasm.

As weeks turned into months, Marco's dedication began to bear fruit. The prototype, once a mere skeleton of wires and metal, took form, its blades designed to mimic the artful curves of nature's own designs. When the day came to test his invention, the town gathered, their collective breath held in suspense.

With the flip of a switch and a gust of wind coaxed from the sea, the turbine came to life, its blades spinning effortlessly, silently, beautifully. The crowd erupted in cheers, and Marco, with tears in his eyes, felt the full weight of his achievement. The long hours, the sacrifice, the single-minded pursuit—it had all led to this moment of triumph.

The impact of Marco's discovery rippled far beyond the shores of Seabreeze Haven. It became a testament to the power of excitement as a catalyst for change, a reminder that passion, when coupled with persistence, could indeed move the world.

In the annals of the town's history, Marco's story remained an inspiration. He was a living example that excitement need not be fleeting or frivolous but could be the very force that propels humanity forward, the wind that fills the sails of innovation and carries us into a brighter future.

VISUALIZATION EXERCISES

Visualization Exercise 1: The Spark of Inspiration

Find a comfortable spot and close your eyes, allowing your breath to become slow and steady. Imagine yourself in a dark space, calm and quiet. Suddenly, a spark of light appears—the embodiment of a new, exciting idea. Watch as this spark grows brighter and transforms into a flame. This flame represents your excitement, your passion. Feel its warmth and energy as it expands, lighting up the space around you. Visualize this energy flowing through you, invigorating every cell in your body, filling you with a sense of eagerness and anticipation for what's to come. Allow yourself to bask in the sensations that excitement brings, and when you're ready, open your eyes, carrying that energetic glow with you.

Visualization Exercise 2: The Pathway of Possibilities

Begin by taking a deep breath and letting it out slowly. Picture yourself standing at the beginning of a path that stretches out before you, meandering through a landscape brimming with potential and opportunities. With each step you take on this path, allow yourself to feel increasingly thrilled by the endless possibilities. Envision the goals and dreams you wish to achieve along this pathway, and with each new step, feel your excitement building. See yourself reaching out to touch these dreams, making them more tangible with your enthusiasm and zest. Let this visualization reinforce the power of positive anticipation in your life.

Visualization Exercise 3: The Soaring Balloon

Sit down and gently close your eyes, focusing on your natural rhythm of breathing. In your mind's eye, see a colorful hot air balloon in an open field, ready for takeoff. This balloon represents your journey toward an exciting goal. Visualize yourself stepping into the basket. As the balloon begins to rise, feel your heart lift with excitement. Higher and higher you climb, soaring toward the clouds. Look down at the world below, growing smaller as you rise above any challenges or doubts. Feel the exhilarating sense of freedom and the thrill of pursuing your aspirations. When you're ready to return, see yourself gently descending, landing softly back to where you started, bringing the excitement and confidence from your journey back into your daily life.

CHANNELING EXCITEMENT TOWARDS POSITIVE OUTCOMES

1. **Goal Setting with Excitement:** Identify goals that genuinely ignite your enthusiasm. Use this excitement as the fuel to propel you toward achieving them. Make sure these goals resonate with your personal values and vision for the future, as alignment is key to maintaining long-term excitement and commitment.

2. **Excitement as Inspiration:** Let excitement be the spark that drives your creativity. Whether it's beginning a new art project, innovating at work, or finding unique solutions to everyday challenges, excitement can be a powerful impetus for creative thinking.

3. **Physical Activity for Energy Management:** Excitement, while energizing, can sometimes feel overwhelming. Engage in physical activities, such as sports or dance, to help channel this surplus energy productively and restore your inner equilibrium.

4. **Excitement Algorithm Reflection:** Take time to reflect on the role excitement plays in your life. Think about the times when you've felt most animated and enthusiastic. What triggered these feelings? Understanding this can help you recreate and sustain excitement in the long term.

5. **Sharing Excitement:** Share your passionate energy with those around you. This not only multiplies the joy but can also lead to collaborative success. By spreading excitement,

you invite others to match your energy, which can enhance group dynamics and lead to collective achievements.

As this chapter concludes, you've learned to welcome excitement and also to direct it constructively. Excitement, when harnessed effectively, can lead to rich experiences, deepened relationships, and the achievement of your most cherished goals. It is an emotion that adds color to the canvas of your life and can be a regular source of inspiration and joy.

18

Fear

Fear is a primal emotion, an intrinsic part of the human experience that serves as a signal of potential danger and prepares us for protective action. In Chapter 18, we approach fear not as an enemy but as a natural response that, when understood, can be managed and overcome. This chapter will guide you through confronting your fears and provide courage-building exercises to empower you to move beyond your apprehensions.

CONFRONTING FEARS: FROM UNDERSTANDING TO OVERCOMING

Understanding our fears is the first step in overcoming them. By recognizing the origins of our fears, whether they are instinctual or learned, we can begin to address them rationally. We'll explore narratives like that of Emily, a teacher who fears public speaking. As she begins to understand the root of her fear, she gradually overcomes it to speak confidently in front of her class.

EMILY

In Seabreeze Haven, where every voice could carry across the gentle tides, Emily's remained a mere whisper in the winds. As a dedicated teacher, her passion for nurturing young minds was as vast as the ocean, but when it came to speaking in front of her class, her voice, usually clear as a bell, would falter and retreat like the shore at low tide.

Emily's fear of public speaking was a shadow that loomed over her, darkening an otherwise bright career. She understood the irony—every day, she stood before a sea of expectant faces, yet the thought of addressing them with authority sent her heart into disarray, her palms into a storm of sweat.

Determined to confront the root of her fear, Emily started a process of self-reflection. She traced the origins of her anxiety to her early years, to a time when a speech gone awry had sown seeds of doubt in her fertile confidence. The embarrassment of that moment had taken root, growing into a gnarled tree of fear that now overshadowed her ability to shine.

Armed with this understanding, Emily sought the guidance of a mentor, Mrs. Hawthorne, a former teacher whose voice had once graced the classrooms of Seabreeze Haven. Mrs. Hawthorne shared her wisdom, teaching Emily techniques to anchor her thoughts and calm her nerves: deep breathing to tame the tempest within and visualization to picture a receptive and engaged audience.

Slowly, Emily began to implement these strategies, standing before her mirror each morning, practicing her lessons with an imagined audience of seagulls and waves. She infused her rehearsals with the enthusiasm she genuinely felt for teaching, allowing her passion to guide her through the fog of fear.

The true test came with the annual school assembly, where Emily was to speak about her innovative teaching methods. As she stepped onto the stage, she felt the familiar flutter of butterflies in her stomach. But this time, she welcomed them as companions. Taking a deep breath, she anchored herself in the present, recalled the faces of her mentor and her supportive students, and began to speak.

To her wonder, her voice did not waver; it sailed across the auditorium, steady and sure. With each sentence, the roots of her fear receded, and in their place grew sprouts of confidence. By the end of her speech, the audience was not only listening but applauding, their faces alight with respect and admiration.

Emily's story of overcoming her fear of public speaking became a lesson she shared with her students—not about the subject matter she taught, but about life itself. She became an example to them that fear, no matter how deep-seated, could be acknowledged, understood, and ultimately mastered.

In Seabreeze Haven, Emily is remembered not as the teacher who once trembled at the podium, but as the educator who taught her students the most valuable lesson of all: that within every fear lies the opportunity for growth, and within every person, the potential to transcend their limitations.

VISUALIZATION EXERCISES

Visualization Exercise 1: The Calm Cove

Sit comfortably, close your eyes, and take a deep breath. Envision yourself standing on the shoreline of a serene cove. The water is still, and the atmosphere is peaceful. Across the cove is a lighthouse, a symbol of guidance and safety. Acknowledge any fears that come to mind as dark clouds in the sky. With each breath, watch the clouds gradually dissipate and the light from the lighthouse grow stronger. Feel the warmth of the light as it reaches you, wrapping you in comfort and courage. As the light becomes brighter, feel your fear losing its power, shrinking away. Take a few moments to bask in this feeling of security and then gently open your eyes, carrying this sense of courage with you.

Visualization Exercise 2: The Staircase of Confidence

Breathe in deeply and imagine yourself at the base of a grand spiraling staircase. This staircase represents your journey through fear toward confidence. Each step is an action or thought that brings you closer to overcoming your fear. Visualize yourself taking one step at a time, steadily climbing with determination and resolve. With each rise, feel your fear diminishing as confidence builds within you. When you reach the top, stand tall and look back down the staircase. Reflect on the courage it took to ascend and the growth you've achieved. Allow yourself to feel proud before you open your eyes and return to the present moment.

Visualization Exercise 3: The Forest of Shadows and Light

Begin by visualizing yourself walking through a dense forest at dusk. Shadows stir around you, each one representing a different fear. As you walk, you hold a lantern that casts a gentle, reassuring glow. Recognize each shadow for what it is: a fear that you can face. With each step forward, shine your light on the shadows, watching them retreat and transform into familiar, harmless shapes. The path ahead clears with the light of your courage, leading you to a clearing bathed in the golden light of dawn. Feel the warmth and safety of the light as the forest behind you becomes bright and inviting. Take a deep breath and carry this light with you as you gently return to your surroundings.

COURAGE-BUILDING EXERCISES

1. **Fear Mapping:** This begins with introspection. Allocate a quiet time to sit and document every fear that surfaces, no matter how small or significant. Look at each fear objectively, categorizing them into what is within and outside your control. By understanding the origins and triggers of each fear, you create a "map" that can help you to address them logically and systematically. Reflect on past experiences. How have these fears affected your decisions, and how might confronting them change your future?

2. **Visualization Techniques:** Visualization is not just about seeing yourself overcoming fear; it's also about feeling the victory and the accompanying emotions. Dedicate time daily to visualize not only the process of facing the fear but also the aftermath—bask in the feelings of triumph and relief. Imagine the sense of freedom and the doors that open

when you're no longer held back by these fears. Such vivid mental rehearsals can reshape your brain's responses to fear, turning imagined scenarios into a blueprint for reality.

3. **Gradual Exposure:** Moving from theory to practice, start with the least intimidating scenarios. Perhaps engage in a mild version of your fear in a safe environment, or role-play a feared situation with a trusted friend. With each small victory, your confidence grows, and what once seemed insurmountable becomes achievable. Journal your experiences after each exposure to track your progress and growth. Seeing your own evolution can be a powerful motivator for continuing the journey.

4. **Support Networks:** Building a robust support system is vital. Open up to others about your journey, sharing not just your fears but also your small wins. A support network can provide perspective, advice, and a safety net when challenges arise. Also, consider joining groups or forums where others share similar fears. Sometimes, seeing someone else overcome their fears can inspire and motivate you to do the same.

5. **Fear Algorithm Reflection:** Establish a regular reflection practice, possibly through journaling or meditation, to assess how you deal with fear. Ask yourself what strategies have been effective and what you've learned from each encounter with fear. Have these strategies allowed you to move forward, or do they need adjustment? Through reflection, you can develop a personalized fear algorithm—a set of principles and actions—that can guide you toward a more fearless life.

You now have a more comprehensive understanding of fear and some practical tools for facing it. The strategies provided will enable you to build courage, reframe your fears as challenges to be met, and transform your relationship with this often-misunderstood emotion. Fear, when confronted with understanding and courage, can become a stimulus for growth and empowerment, leading to a life lived with greater confidence and freedom.

19

Horror

Horror, a potent form of fear often associated with intense shock, disgust, or repulsion, can leave a lasting impact on our psyche. In this chapter, we confront the emotion of horror, exploring its effects and how to recover from the paralysis it can induce. You'll find coping strategies to help you process and move past horrific experiences, restoring a sense of safety and normalcy.

THE SHOCK OF HORROR AND ITS AFTERMATH

Horror can be experienced in various forms, from witnessing a traumatic event to consuming frightening media. It's an emotion that can challenge our sense of security and understanding of the world. We'll examine the immediate and lingering effects of horror through the experiences of individuals like Alex, a first responder who faces the aftermath of natural disasters, and the measures he takes to heal from the vicarious trauma he encounters.

ALEX

In the resilient heart of Seabreeze Haven, Alex was a steadfast presence, a first responder whose courage was a beacon in the tempest. He was a living example of the human capacity for bravery as he stood on the front lines whenever nature's fury descended upon the town or the surrounding areas.

Alex had chosen this path knowing the risks, aware of the horrors he might witness in the wake of earthquakes, hurricanes, or floods. Yet nothing could have fully prepared him for the emotional toll of such catastrophic events. The devastation he faced, the suffering he witnessed, etched deep grooves of vicarious trauma into his psyche.

Despite the horrors, Alex's commitment never faltered. But he recognized the importance of healing from the trauma to continue serving his community effectively. So he began to employ a variety of self-care measures, each one a step toward hope and recovery.

He found solace in the solidarity of his colleagues, those who understood the silent burden he carried. They gathered after each mission, not just to debrief on the practicalities but to share their experiences and support each other's emotional well-being.

Alex also turned to the therapeutic embrace of nature, spending time in the tranquil environments around Seabreeze Haven. He would walk along the beach or through the forests, allowing the rhythmic sounds of the waves and the whispering trees to soothe his mind.

Mindfulness became a cornerstone of his daily routine. Through meditation, Alex learned to observe his thoughts and emotions without judgment, to sit with them and then let them go, like leaves on a river, acknowledging their presence but not letting them anchor him down.

He also sought professional support, engaging in sessions with a therapist who specialized in trauma. These sessions became a space for Alex to unpack the weight of his experiences, to vocalize the horror without fear of burdening others.

As he implemented these measures, Alex began to feel the grip of the vicarious trauma loosen. He discovered a newfound resilience within himself, an ability to witness the aftermath of disasters without letting the darkness seep into his soul.

Alex's story of facing horror and finding ways to heal is a powerful narrative shared in Seabreeze Haven. It serves as a reminder of the strength that lies in vulnerability, the courage in seeking help, and the real impact of taking steps to heal oneself. Alex is not just a hero for the lives he saves in the wake of disasters; he represents hope for the enduring spirit of all who confront the shadows and find their way back to light.

VISUALIZATION EXERCISES

Visualization Exercise 1: The Sanctuary of Light

Sit in a quiet place where you feel safe. Close your eyes and take a deep breath. Envision a sphere of warm, protective light enveloping you. This light is your sanctuary, impenetrable and calming. Inside this space, acknowledge any images or feelings of horror that come to mind, then visualize them fading away as they touch the edges of the light. They cannot reach you here. The warmth of the light grows stronger with each breath, reinforcing your sense of security. Feel the serenity and safety surrounding you, and when you're ready, gently open your eyes, carrying this sense of protection with you.

Visualization Exercise 2: The Tree of Resilience

Imagine yourself walking in a peaceful forest. You come across an ancient, sturdy tree—it represents your inner strength and resilience. Sit under this tree and lean against its strong trunk. Visualize any recent horrors or fears as storm clouds overhead. Watch as the tree's leaves absorb the storm, turning the clouds into clear skies. Feel the support and stability of the tree, and know that like the tree, you can weather any storm. Take a moment to appreciate the resilience you possess, and when you feel ready, rise and leave the forest, feeling grounded and centered.

Visualization Exercise 3: The Dissolving Mist

Breathe deeply in a comfortable position. Picture yourself standing on a hill at dawn, the valley below filled with a thick mist that symbolizes the horror and trauma you've experienced. As the sun rises, its rays begin to touch the mist. Slowly, the mist starts to dissolve under the gentle warmth of the sunlight. With each ray of light, the mist thins out, taking away the intense images and emotions with it. Witness the landscape becoming clear, revealing the beauty of the valley—a metaphor for your clarity and peace of mind. As the mist disappears completely, affirm to yourself the passing nature of all experiences. When you feel at peace, bring yourself back to the present.

COPING STRATEGIES FOR HORRIFIC EXPERIENCES

1. **Immediate Grounding Techniques:** The first and foremost step is to ground yourself. Techniques such as deep breathing, sensory focus exercises, or grounding objects can be invaluable. These methods anchor you to the present moment, diverting your mind from reliving the horror. By focusing on your breath or detailing the environment around you, you're telling your nervous system that you're safe, allowing your body to calm down from the fight or flight response.

2. **Trauma-Informed Care:** Educate yourself on what constitutes trauma-informed care. Understanding its principles can aid in identifying the right kind of support, be it through therapy, community groups, or other professional services. It's about creating a plan that recognizes the impact of trauma and helps to rebuild a sense of control and empowerment. Seek professionals who specialize in trauma and can guide you through the healing process with sensitivity and understanding.

3. **Artistic Expression:** Art offers a non-verbal outlet where words may fail. Through painting, writing, music, or any other form of art, you can express and process the complex emotions that come with horror. This expression not only serves as a release but can also help to make sense of what you've gone through. It doesn't need to be shared or even be

"good" by any standard; it just needs to be honest and true to your feelings.

4. **Building a Supportive Community:** Finding or building a community can significantly impact your healing journey. This community can be made up of friends, family, support groups, or online communities where people share similar experiences. Within this safe space, you can trade stories, offer and receive advice, and feel a sense of belonging. The shared experience of horror can forge strong bonds that become a source of continual support and comfort.

5. **Horror Algorithm Reflection:** Develop an "algorithm" for managing the aftermath of horror by reflecting on what coping mechanisms work for you. This could mean setting aside time for self-reflection, journaling about your experiences, or creating art. By understanding how you process these events, you can create a tailored approach to handling them in the future. Regularly revisiting and adjusting your horror algorithm ensures it remains effective as you grow and your needs change.

By the close of Chapter 19, your understanding of horror's deep emotional impact and a set of tools to aid in recovery allows you to confront the aftermath of horror with grace, employing coping strategies that support healing and resilience. Take this time to contemplate on the human spirit's ability to endure and eventually find peace, even after the most harrowing experiences.

20

Interest

Interest is the spark that fuels our curiosity, driving us to explore, learn, and engage deeply with the world around us. In Chapter 20, we focus on cultivating a life enriched by curiosity and interest. We look at how fostering interest can lead to continuous personal growth and a rewarding life. This chapter provides prompts to stimulate curiosity and deepen engagement with our passions as well as the environment we inhabit.

CULTIVATING A LIFE OF CURIOSITY AND INTEREST

A cultivated sense of interest has the power to transform mundane tasks into adventures and to turn passing moments into opportunities for discovery. We'll hear the story of Nadia, an urban planner whose interest in sustainable cities leads her to travel and bring innovative ideas back to her hometown. Her curiosity becomes a career-driving force, leading to transformative projects that benefit her community.

NADIA

In Seabreeze Haven, a coastal town where the future was as important as its heritage, Nadia emerged as a visionary urban planner. Her interest in sustainable cities was more than a profession; it was a calling that drew her across continents, seeking the secrets of harmony between urban life and environmental stewardship.

Nadia's journey began with a scholarship to attend a conference on green urban planning. There, she encountered minds as fertile as the wetlands back home, ideas as diverse as the coral in Seabreeze Haven's bay. She absorbed lessons from cities that rose high yet left light footprints, where rooftops flourished with gardens and roads pulsed with clean energy.

With each city she visited, Nadia collected strategies: water reclamation systems from arid regions, waste-to-energy innovations from bustling metropolises, and community gardens that turned food deserts into oases. Her curiosity was insatiable, her notepads filled with sketches and notes, her mind always whirring with the potential for application back home.

Upon her return to Seabreeze Haven, Nadia found herself at the heart of a growing movement for change. She proposed bold initiatives, like the adaptation of old buildings into vertical farms and the installation of tidal energy converters to harness the power of the ocean that cradled the town.

Skepticism met some of her ideas like sea cliffs facing the waves, resistant and worn. But Nadia's passion was a gale that could erode the hardest stone. Her conviction was infectious, her knowledge undeniable. One by one, projects began to take root, starting with a pilot for rainwater harvesting in the public park, which bloomed into a lush community hub.

As her plans came to fruition, Seabreeze Haven transformed. The air grew cleaner, the energy greener, and the people healthier. Nadia's curiosity-driven career spoke to the town's potential, a story of how one person's interest could spark a collective awakening to the value of sustainability.

In the annals of Seabreeze Haven, Nadia's story is told with pride—a tale of a hometown girl who ventured out into the world and returned to create a future where the town not only survives but thrives. Her legacy is seen in the very layout of the streets, in the verdant walls of buildings, and in the consciousness of her community.

VISUALIZATION EXERCISES

Visualization Exercise 1: The Garden of Wonders

Close your eyes and take a deep breath in. Picture yourself in a vast, lush garden where each plant and flower represents a topic or subject that piques your interest. Allow yourself to wander through this garden, noticing the colors, the scents, and how each plant makes you feel. Some may draw you in closer, inviting you to explore further. As you walk, feel your curiosity grow. Reach out and touch a leaf or a petal, feeling the knowledge it represents soak into your fingertips, filling you with understanding and excitement. Spend a few moments with each plant that draws your attention, letting the joy of learning and discovery fill you up. When you're ready, gently open your eyes, bringing back with you the sense of wonder and eagerness to explore and learn more about the things that interest you.

Visualization Exercise 2: The Library of Possibilities

Imagine you are entering a colossal library with infinite books, each representing different facets of your interests. Visualize yourself exploring the aisles, feeling the quiet hum of potential knowledge surrounding you. Pull out a book that catches your eye, feeling the weight of its wisdom in your hands. Flip through the pages, seeing words and images that fascinate you. Each book you look at deepens your interest and passion for learning. When you feel a sense of fulfillment and intellectual curiosity, place the book back on the shelf, knowing you can return any time. Slowly bring your attention back to the present, feeling enriched and inspired.

Visualization Exercise 3: The River of Inquiry

Sit quietly, breathing in a rhythm that feels natural and calming. Picture yourself beside a gently flowing river. This river flows with questions and a thirst for knowledge. Watch as the water flows, sparkling with potential answers and insights. Visualize yourself dipping your hands into the water, feeling the cool flow of curiosity through your fingers. With each question that comes to mind, imagine the river branching off into streams, leading you toward the answers. Feel the excitement of following these streams, discovering new paths of understanding. Allow yourself to be guided by this flow of inquisitiveness, and when you are ready, step back onto the riverbank, refreshed and invigorated with a renewed love for learning and exploration.

PROMPTS TO DEEPEN KNOWLEDGE AND ENGAGEMENT

1. **Curiosity Journaling:** Cultivating a sense of wonder about the world starts with attention. Keep a journal where you note down your curiosities, be they fleeting questions or profound inquiries. It doesn't just record your thoughts; it also encourages you to follow through on finding answers, turning curiosity into a driving force for personal development.

2. **Diversify Information Sources:** Broadening your informational horizon can enrich your life in unexpected ways. Venture into reading materials you wouldn't normally pick up, listen to podcasts that challenge your viewpoints, and join groups where discussions thrive on diverse perspectives. This broadens your knowledge and can also refine your critical thinking and empathy.

3. **Skill Exploration:** Encourage yourself to learn new skills or delve into hobbies that intrigue you. Step beyond the familiar—whether it's learning a language, drawing, writing a poem or gardening.. It's about the joy of learning and the satisfaction that comes from growth, not necessarily mastery.

4. **Engagement Challenges:** Set yourself weekly challenges that prompt you to interact with new ideas and communities. Attend a workshop, volunteer, or start a project that aligns with an emerging interest. Such engagements not only enhance knowledge but also build networks and open doors to opportunities.

5. **Interest Algorithm Reflection:** Reflect on your interests regularly and recognize patterns. Do certain topics consis-

tently draw you in? What subjects do you engage with deeply, and which ones do you skim? By understanding your interest patterns, you can create a personalized algorithm that helps guide your learning and engagement strategies, ensuring that your interests not only stay alive but also evolve.

Through these exercises, you are learning to appreciate the role of interest in leading a vibrant and dynamic life, and you also now possess a variety of tactics to sustain and expand your realms of interest. This chapter guides you to remain open to new experiences, to question, and to connect, building a life that is constantly enriched by the pursuit of knowledge and engagement.

21

Joy

J oy is a deep sense of happiness and fulfillment that can brighten our lives and uplift our spirits. In this chapter, we explore the pursuit of joy through life's simple pleasures and the importance of recognizing and cultivating these moments. You'll find practical activities to track and create joy, encouraging you to actively seek and cherish the moments that make life vibrant.

THE PURSUIT OF JOY IN LIFE'S SIMPLE PLEASURES

Joy can be found in the smallest moments: a warm cup of tea on a cold morning, the laughter of a child, or the scent of rain on dry earth. It's these simple pleasures that often provide the most authentic experiences of joy. We'll introduce you to people like Oliver, a gardener who finds immense joy in the quiet process of tending to his plants, and Elena, a musician who discovers joy in the daily ritual of morning melodies.

OLIVER

In the heart of Seabreeze Haven, amidst the hum of waves and the whispers of the coastal breeze, there was a garden that was a riot of colors and fragrances, a living canvas painted daily by Oliver, the town's gardener. His love for the earth and its blooms was not merely a duty; it was a wellspring of joy that ran as deep as the roots of the oldest tree in his care.

Oliver's days began with the first kiss of sunlight over the horizon as he stepped into his garden with a sense of reverence. His fingers, weathered and wise, worked the soil, coaxing life from the earth with the tenderness of a sculptor. To him, each seed was a promise, each sapling evidence of life's relentless urge to grow and thrive.

The garden was Oliver's sanctuary, where the symphony of nature was the only soundtrack and time was marked by the growth of the plants rather than the ticking of a clock. The rustle of the leaves was his conversation, the bloom of a new flower his celebration. It was in these quiet moments, with dirt under his fingernails and the sun warming his back, that Oliver found a joy so profound it often left him without words.

His garden became a place for those seeking solace and a moment of peace. Children watched in wonder as butterflies danced from flower to flower, and adults found themselves transported back to the innocence of their youth as they wandered the paths Oliver had so lovingly crafted.

Yet it was not only the beauty of the garden that brought joy to Oliver and those who visited. It was the knowledge that this patch of earth was a haven for all creatures, big and small, and that in nurturing his garden, Oliver was nurturing life itself. His dedication to the cycles of nature, to the dance of the seasons, was a quiet devotion that resonated with a world that often moved too fast.

As the years passed, Oliver's hair silvered like the dew on morning petals, but his joy never waned. His garden grew richer, telling of the care imbued in every leaf, every petal, every inch of soil. In Seabreeze Haven, Oliver's garden became a legend, a place where joy grew in abundance, where the beauty of life was celebrated every day, with every bloom.

ELENA

In the cozy seaside town of Seabreeze Haven, mornings were greeted not just by the sunrise but by the soul-stirring melodies that flowed from Elena's open window. She was the town's beloved musician, a virtuoso whose life was a symphony of notes and nuances, rhythms and rhymes.

For Elena, each day began with a sacred ritual. As the first light of dawn painted the sky in strokes of pink and gold, she would sit at her piano, her fingers poised gracefully above the keys, her heart open and receptive to the new day's song. This was her time, her moment of communion with the silent muse that visited her with the promise of a fresh melody.

The music that filled her mornings was spontaneous, an unbridled expression of the joy she found in the simple act of creation.

There were no audiences to impress, no critics to fear, just the pure delight of discovery as her hands danced across the keys, conjuring harmonies and chords that echoed the rhythm of the awakening world.

The townspeople of Seabreeze Haven often paused in their morning routines, cups of coffee in hand, as the sweet serenade of Elena's piano reached their ears. Her music became a staple of their daily lives, a reminder to find happiness in the ordinary, to cherish the quotidian miracles that so often go unnoticed.

Elena's morning melodies were not compositions to be recorded or performed on grand stages. They were ephemeral gifts to the day, offerings of sound that were as much a part of the morning as the chorus of the seabirds or the gentle lapping of the waves against the shore.

It was in these fleeting moments of musical alchemy that Elena discovered a deep sense of fulfillment and purpose. Her joy did not stem from accolades or acclaim but from the intimate personal connection she forged with her music each new day.

As time went by, Elena's ritual never wavered. Her music aged with her, each note part of the life she lived and loved. And in Seabreeze Haven, her legacy would resonate long after the final note faded, a timeless echo of the joy that can be found in each dawn's quiet melody.

VISUALIZATION EXERCISES

Visualization Exercise 1: The Melody of Happiness

Sit back, relax, and close your eyes. Begin by taking slow, deep breaths, inhaling peace and exhaling any tension. Envision yourself in a sunlit field, surrounded by wildflowers dancing in the breeze. In the distance, a soft, inviting melody plays—the sound of your own personal joy. With each note, feel a wave of happiness wash over you, starting from your toes and rising all the way to the crown of your head. Allow this melody to move you, to fill your spirit with lightness and laughter. Dance freely in the field, embracing the music as it intertwines with the essence of your being. When you're ready, carry this tune back with you, letting it linger in your heart as you gently open your eyes.

Visualization Exercise 2: The Bubble of Bliss

Inhale deeply, and as you exhale, visualize a bubble forming around you. This bubble is filled with a warm, golden light, representing the joy within you. See yourself lifting off the ground, carried by this bubble through skies painted with the hues of dawn. As you float, look down to see the stresses and worries of life becoming smaller, losing their power over you. Feel the freedom and weightlessness of this joyful journey. Soar above mountains and valleys, and with each breath, let your joy grow and expand until it fills the bubble completely. When you feel suffused with happiness, allow the bubble to gently descend and settle back to earth. Step out, filled with a renewed sense of joy, ready to approach your day with a light heart.

Visualization Exercise 3: The Fountain of Joy

Close your eyes and picture a tranquil garden where a fountain of crystal-clear water stands. This fountain is special; it springs from your innermost feelings of joy. Watch as the water cascades, sparkling in the sunlight, and hear its cheerful bubbling. Approach the fountain and cup your hands, letting the cool water gather in your palms. Bring your hands to your face, feeling the refreshing sensation as you splash the water on your skin. With every drop, feel more invigorated, more filled with life's simple joys. Let the sight and sound of the fountain remind you of the abundance of happiness that can spring forth from within, no matter where you are or what you're doing. Sit by the fountain for a few more moments, then slowly open your eyes, feeling joyful and refreshed.

JOY-TRACKING AND CREATION ACTIVITIES

1. **Joy Algorithm Reflection:** Dedicate time to introspect on what truly brings you joy. Reflecting can help you identify and seek out these moments or activities more consciously, making joy a regular part of your life rather than a fleeting emotion.

2. **Gratitude Practices:** Gratitude can transform your outlook on life, turning ordinary moments into treasures. Start or end your day by writing down what you are grateful for, be it the warmth of the sun or a kind gesture from a stranger. This habit can significantly uplift your mood and bring a sustained sense of happiness.

3. **Mindfulness Moments:** Incorporate mindfulness exercises into your routine to enhance your capacity for joy. This might be through meditation, taking a mindful walk, or

simply breathing deeply and savoring the moment. Mindfulness anchors you in the now, allowing you to fully engage with and cherish joyous experiences.

4. **Creative Expression:** Creativity is a powerful conduit for joy. Engage in creative pursuits that resonate with you, from painting to playing music to writing poetry. These activities not only bring satisfaction and fulfillment but also allow you to express and share your joy with the world.

5. **Social Connection:** Strong social ties are fundamental to experiencing joy. Nurture your relationships by spending quality time with friends and family, participating in community events, or helping others through volunteer work. The joy found in these connections is reciprocal and greatly life-enhancing.

By consciously incorporating these practices into your life, you build a reservoir of joy that sustains you through challenging times and enriches the good times, creating a life that feels fulfilling and complete.

As this chapter draws to a close, you know more about the role of joy in your life and have gained some practical methods for seeking and recognizing joy every day. You are learning that joy does not always come from grand achievements or major life events; it often whispers in the quiet corners of your everyday experiences. This chapter empowers you to make joy an active part of your life, transforming ordinary days into a series of joyful discoveries.

22

Love

L ove, in its many forms, is a profound and multifaceted emotion that can encompass affection, compassion, and deep bonds. In the chapter that follows, we delve into the depths of love, exploring how it enriches our lives and connects us to others. Discover practices to help you open your heart to love, foster its growth, and navigate the complexities of one of life's most powerful emotions.

EXPLORING THE DEPTHS OF LOVE

Love can be as quiet as the comfort of a trusted friend or as exhilarating as the passion of a new romance. We explore the different expressions of love, from platonic to romantic, self-love to altruistic love, and how each enriches our experience. Through the story of Mia and Carlos, a couple whose love evolves over decades, adapting and deepening, readers will see the enduring nature of love and its capacity to grow and change.

Kassidy and Carlos

In the town of Seabreeze Haven, where the sea ebbs and flows with the constancy of time itself, there lived a couple whose love was as enduring as the ocean's rhythm. Kassidy and Carlos met in their youth, their affection sprouting like the spring's first bloom under the nurturing sun of the seaside.

Their love was not a fiery passion that flared and fizzed, but rather like a deep current in the tranquil waters of Seabreeze Haven, steady and sure. As they made their way through life's seasons together, their love was a vessel that weathered storms and savored calm seas, always steering them home to each other.

In the early days, their love was a canvas of bright colors, bold strokes of joy in shared adventures and dreams. They danced through days of sunshine, their laughter mingling with the gulls' cries, as they planned a future as wide and open as the horizon.

But love, like the sea, changes its nature. With time, the bright canvas deepened in hue, the strokes of joy interspersed with the gentle shading of challenges faced and overcome. They learned that love's true depth is found in the quiet moments: the soft word in times of doubt, the steady hand when the ground shakes, the shared glance that speaks volumes in the silence.

Kassidy and Carlos nurtured their love as they did their seaside garden, with patience and care, knowing that the most beautiful blooms take time to unfold. As they grew older, their bond deepened, roots entwining so thoroughly that it became impossible to tell where one ended and the other began.

Through the decades, their love evolved. The electric thrill of youthful affection matured into a partnership, the kind that speaks through the soft squeeze of a hand or the warmth of a shared blanket on cool evenings. Their love evidenced that, while people grow and change, the heart's capacity for love grows and changes with them.

In Seabreeze Haven, Kassidy and Carlos became known as an example of love's enduring nature. Their story inspired the young lovers who walked hand in hand along the beach, the new parents cradling life's fresh beginning, and the elderly couples who saw in Kassidy and Carlos the reflection of their own lives' loves.

Their love story, spanning decades, was living proof that love, in all its forms, is a force that endures. It adapts and deepens, resilient in the face of life's relentless tides, able to grow and change.

VISUALIZATION EXERCISES

Visualization Exercise 1: The Heart's Garden

Close your eyes and envision yourself entering a vibrant garden, the garden of your heart, where every plant and flower symbolizes the love you have experienced and given in your life. Notice the variety—the budding new loves, the mature, steadfast oaks of long-term bonds, and the resilient perennials that return year after year. Walk along the path of this garden, tending to each plant, appreciating their unique beauty and place in your heart. As you water and care for them, feel the love within you grow and radiate outward. Take deep breaths, and with each exhale, spread this love to those around you, feeling your connection and a deep gratitude for these relationships.

Visualization Exercise 2: The Connecting Thread

In a quiet space, take a few deep breaths to center yourself. Imagine a thread of light that originates from your heart and extends outward. This thread represents the love that connects you to a significant person in your life. Visualize this thread reaching out to them, wherever they are, and see them receiving this love, acknowledging it, and sending their love back to you through the same thread. Feel the strength of this bond and the exchange of pure, unconditional love. Sit with this connection, allowing the feelings of love and peace to fill you up.

Visualization Exercise 3: The Ripple of Love

Sit comfortably and picture a still pond in front of you. This pond represents your capacity to love and be loved. See a pebble, symbolizing your love, drop into the center of the pond. Watch as ripples emanate from where the pebble entered the water, traveling farther and farther out. With each ripple, feel your love expanding, reaching more of those you care for—family, friends, even strangers. Allow the expanding ripples to symbolize the growing impact of your love on the world. Reflect on the joy and warmth this brings to you and those touched by the ripples of your love. When you feel filled with this love, gently open your eyes, carrying this loving energy into your day.

PRACTICES TO OPEN THE HEART

1. **Loving-Kindness Meditation:** This practice involves sending wishes of love and kindness to yourself, loved ones, acquaintances, and even those with whom you may have difficulty. By doing so, you open your heart to the flow of compassion, which can transform your perspective on life and relationships.

2. **Affectionate Communication:** Make it a habit to communicate your affection and gratitude to those around you. This could be through words, acts of service, or small gestures that convey appreciation. Such practices enrich your relationships and contribute to a loving environment.

3. **Heart-Opening Yoga Poses:** Engage in yoga practices that focus on opening the heart chakra, such as backbends or chest-opening poses. These poses not only improve physical flexibility but are also believed to encourage the release of emotional blockages, encouraging openness and receptivity to love.

4. **Emotional Vulnerability:** Allow yourself to be vulnerable with people you trust. Sharing your true feelings, fears, and hopes can lead to deeper connections. Vulnerability is a strength that, when embraced, can lead to a more meaningful experience of love and intimacy in your relationships.

5. **Love Algorithm Reflection:** Reflect on how you experience and express love in your life. Consider what actions and attitudes help you feel more connected and which ones create distance. Use this reflection to create a personal "algorithm" for love that aligns with your values and relationship goals.

Love, in all its forms, requires effort and intention. By integrating these practices into your life, you'll find that love is more than just an emotion; it is a state of being that you can nurture and grow.

By the end of Chapter 22, you have awakened an understanding of love in all its diversity, and discovered a set of practices to help foster and express this essential emotion. Love is not just a feeling but an action, a choice that can be made every day, in countless ways. This chapter invites you to embrace love's transformative power and to open your heart to its potential in every aspect of life.

23

Nostalgia

N ostalgia is a bittersweet yearning for the past, often evoking a mixture of emotions ranging from happiness to melancholy. In this chapter, we explore the complex nature of nostalgia, understanding it as more than mere reminiscence. It is a powerful emotional state that can connect us with our identity and shared history. We'll also introduce reflective practices that can help us appreciate and learn from our nostalgic moments.

NOSTALGIA: THE BITTER SWEETNESS OF THE PAST

Nostalgia allows us to revisit the warmth of past experiences and the lessons they've imparted. This emotional journey can reinforce connections to people, places, and times that have shaped who we are. Through the story of Grace, a grandmother who sifts through old letters to relive the joys and trials of her youth, we see how nostalgia serves as a bridge between past and present, offering comfort and a sense of continuity.

GRACE

In Seabreeze Haven, nestled among the warm hues of memory and the sweet fragrance of time gone by, lived Grace, a grandmother whose gentle hands held the wisdom of years. Her attic was a treasure trove of the past, a sanctuary where cardboard boxes overflowed with the yellowed pages of old letters, each a fragment of her life's story.

Grace, in the autumn of her years, found a quiet joy in revisiting these paper memories. It was a ritual she cherished, a voyage back to the days of her vigorous youth, to the moments of laughter and tears, of beginnings and farewells. Each letter was a thread, woven into the fabric of who she had become, each word a whisper of the girl she once was.

With delicate fingers, she would extract a letter from the pile, unfold it, and smooth out its creases, as if tenderly caressing the face of a long-lost friend. The ink, faded but still legible, brought back the voices of those she loved—some who had taken different paths, some who had journeyed beyond where time could reach.

Through these letters, she relived her first dance under the stars, the heartache of a wartime goodbye, the excitement of newfound love, and the pride of motherhood. They spoke of an era when love was poured onto paper, not tapped on screens, when waiting for the postman was a daily thrill, and when news traveled slowly, allowing anticipation to build and savoring to last.

Nostalgia, for Grace, was not a longing to return to those days, but a comforting embrace that linked the past to the present. It was in these moments of reflection that she found continuity in the ebb and flow of life, a reassurance that though the world spins forward, the past remains, cradled in the corners of our hearts.

As her grandchildren would visit, drawn by curiosity, Grace shared her stories with them, bridging generations. The past became a living thing, not just in her retelling but in the lessons it imparted—about resilience, about cherishing the moment, about the endurance of love.

In Seabreeze Haven, Grace's nostalgia was a well from which wisdom was drawn, quenching the thirst for connection in a world often racing ahead. Her legacy was in the memories she kept alive but also in the understanding that while time is a current that carries us, our past is the anchor that offers stability and direction.

VISUALIZATION EXERCISES

Visualization Exercise 1: Memory Lane

Sit comfortably and close your eyes. Take a deep breath in, and as you exhale, imagine yourself walking down a beautiful tree-lined path. This is your Memory Lane. With each step, notice a photo or an item from your past appearing along the path, representing a happy and cherished moment. Pick up these memories, hold them, and relive the emotions they stir within you. Hear the laughter, feel the warmth, and smell the scents of those times. Let these feelings fill you with a sense of joy and connection to your past. When you're ready, gently place the memories back along the path and carry the warmth and happiness they've reignited in you back into the present moment as you open your eyes.

Visualization Exercise 2: The Attic of the Past

Breathe in deeply and let your breath carry you to the attic of an old, familiar house—your mind's repository of the past. Here, amid the soft glow of dust motes in sunlight, are trunks filled with keepsakes and mementos. Open a trunk and lift out objects one by one, each evoking a different period of your life. Feel the textures and let the associated emotions wash over you. With each item, allow yourself to be transported to that time, experiencing the joy, the learning, and even the bittersweet tinge of times gone by. When you feel a sense of completion, carefully place the items back, knowing these memories continue to shape the narrative of who you are. Take a deep breath and return to the present, bringing with you a continuity of self.

Visualization Exercise 3: The River of Time

Imagine yourself sitting by a gentle, flowing river. This river represents the passing of time. Watch as leaves float by on its surface; each leaf is a memory from your past. Some are vivid and colorful, others more faded. Reach out and touch a leaf, allowing yourself to be fully immersed in the memory it represents. Feel the emotions, hear the sounds, and see the sights from this moment in time. As the leaf continues to float down the river, acknowledge the beauty of this memory and how it has contributed to the river's richness. When you're ready, stand up and step back from the riverbank, filled with a sense of peace and understanding of how your past experiences flow into the person you are today. Open your eyes, feeling grounded in the present but enriched by the nostalgia of your journey.

REFLECTING AND INCORPORATING NOSTALGIC MOMENTS

1. **Nostalgic Journeys:** Dive into your old photo albums, listen to music from your past, or look at family heirlooms. Allow yourself to feel the emotions and memories they bring up. It's more than just reminiscing; it's about understanding how these memories shaped you. Document the feelings and insights that come up in a journal to create a narrative of your personal history.

2. **Sensory Triggers:** Use your senses to trigger nostalgic memories. Maybe it's the aroma of a dish that takes you back to your grandmother's kitchen or a song that reminds you of your first dance. Reflect on these experiences and consider what they bring out in you—joy, longing, insight, or perhaps inspiration.

3. **Writing Letters to the Past:** Write letters to your past self or to people who have been significant in your life. This is a therapeutic way to thank, forgive, or simply acknowledge the events of your life. Such letters can be an effective way to connect with parts of yourself and others that you may have lost touch with over time.

4. **Nostalgia Algorithm Reflection:** Reflect on how you engage with nostalgia. Are there patterns in the memories you revisit? Do certain times of the year trigger a longing for the past? Understanding your "nostalgia algorithm" can help you harness these feelings positively, to appreciate the present and look forward to the future.

5. **Balanced Reminiscing:** While it's delightful to look back, it's important to stay grounded in the present. Use your nostalgic experiences to appreciate where you've come from

and the growth you've achieved. Let these memories inform your current life by inspiring you to create new experiences that future you will look back on fondly.

By approaching nostalgia in this balanced way, you can enjoy the warmth of past memories while using them as a springboard for continuous personal growth and present-day satisfaction.

You are discovering an appreciation for the role of nostalgia in shaping your emotional landscape and developing a set of reflective tools to enrich your understanding of yourself through your past. This chapter honors nostalgia as a natural and enriching part of life, inviting you to engage with it in ways that affirm your life's journey and current path.

24

Relief

R elief is the emotional release that comes when a burden is lifted, a threat is removed, or a challenge is overcome. It's a breath of fresh air, a feeling of weight being taken off our shoulders. In Chapter 24, we examine the various contexts in which relief can manifest and how this feeling of release can be a source of renewal and reassurance. You'll learn techniques to not only evoke the sensation of relief but also to deeply appreciate and extend its beneficial effects.

The Sigh of Relief: Understanding Release

Understanding the mechanisms of relief helps us recognize it as a natural response to the resolution of stress or fear. It can follow moments of intense pressure or anxiety, like the end of a taxing project, or it can be the quiet realization that a worry was unfounded. We'll tell the story of Adrian, a disaster response leader who, after days of intense work during a flood, experiences intense relief when the waters recede and families can return home.

Adrian

In the wake of relentless rain that had painted Seabreeze Haven in shades of despair, Adrian stood as a pillar of strength and resilience. As the leader of the disaster response team, he shouldered the burden of hope for the entire town. His days were long, arduous, and soaked not just by the deluge from the heavens but also by the sweat of his exertions and the tears of those he comforted.

Adrian and his team worked tirelessly, orchestrating rescues, shoring up sandbag defenses, and providing the essentials of survival to the displaced. Sleep was an elusive companion, and the haunting worry for the safety of the community was a constant shadow, darkening even the briefest moments of rest.

The waters, like an unwelcome visitor, had crept into homes and lives, leaving a trail of loss and uncertainty. Adrian felt each family's pain acutely, carrying their stories with him as he braved the treacherous currents that had overtaken the streets of his beloved town.

Then, after days that seemed to stretch into an uncertain eternity, the rains began to taper. The clouds that had hung so heavily parted to reveal glimpses of blue sky, a promise that the storm had passed. As the waters receded, revealing the scars upon the land, Adrian allowed himself a moment to watch, to witness the literal ebbing away of crisis.

It was then that relief washed over him—a powerful, overwhelming wave, not of water, but of emotion. It cleansed away the fatigue, the dread, the relentless tension that had become his constant companions. This relief was a balm to his weary soul as he watched residents tentatively, then joyfully, return to their homes.

The relief was tinged with the knowledge that the return was just the beginning of recovery. There would be repairs, both structural and emotional, but the community of Seabreeze Haven was ready to face the challenge, fortified by the unity and compassion that had been reinforced through the ordeal.

In the weeks that followed, as Seabreeze Haven slowly stitched itself back together, Adrian's relief matured into a quiet pride for the resilience of his town. The shared relief became a bonding agent, stronger than the floodwaters. It was an example of the human spirit's capacity to rise, to rebuild, and to find gratitude in the return to normalcy.

Adrian's story of relief, of the calm after the storm, was a reminder that even the deepest floods recede, and from them, the seeds of renewal and hope can sprout.

VISUALIZATION EXERCISES

Visualization Exercise 1: The Dissipating Storm

Find a comfortable position and close your eyes. Take a few deep, slow breaths, and imagine yourself standing in the middle of a storm. The winds are strong, the rain is pouring, and you're holding a shield that's been weighed down by the onslaught. With every breath you take, visualize the storm getting weaker, the clouds starting to part, and the sun peeking through. Feel the weight on your shield becoming lighter, the water running off its edges. The air is fresher now, the storm has passed, and you are still standing, resilient. Feel a sense of relief flood your body as you realize that you're safe and that the worst is over. Hold on to this feeling of lightness and calm as you slowly open your eyes.

Visualization Exercise 2: The Burdened Balloons

Breathe in deeply, and as you breathe out, picture all of your worries, stresses, and fears as heavy balloons tied to your hands. See them in detail—the color, the texture, and the way they pull down on your arms. Now, one by one, untie these balloons and let them go. Watch as they float away into the sky, getting smaller and smaller until they disappear completely. With each balloon you release, feel a sense of relief growing inside you. Your arms are lighter, and your body is free from the heaviness. Stay in this moment of release as long as you need. When you feel ready, gently bring your focus back to the present, feeling renewed and at peace.

Visualization Exercise 3: The Healing Waters

Envision yourself standing barefoot at the edge of a peaceful lake. The water is still, reflecting the clear skies above. As you step into the lake, imagine that the water has the power to wash away all tension and stress. With each step deeper, feel the waters drawing out the fatigue, the worry, and replacing it with a soothing, comforting sense of relief. Walk until you're waist-deep, take a deep breath, and then submerge yourself fully, letting the water envelop you in its embrace. Hold your breath for a moment, then rise back to the surface, feeling a sense of release as you break through into the air, refreshed and cleansed. When you're ready, walk back onto the shore, feeling light and relieved, and open your eyes to the world around you.

TECHNIQUES TO EVOKE AND APPRECIATE RELIEF

1. **Mindful Breathing:** Learn to use breathing techniques that emulate your body's instinctive reactions to feelings of relief. This method involves slow, deep breaths that help center your mind, grounding you in a peaceful state and alleviating stress.

2. **Progressive Muscle Relaxation:** This technique teaches you to identify tension within your body and release it progressively. By tensing and then relaxing different muscle groups, you mirror the physical sensation of relief, which can, in turn, induce emotional tranquility.

3. **Problem-Solving Strategies:** Equip yourself with effective problem-solving methods. By breaking down issues into manageable pieces and methodically addressing each one, the resolution of stress factors becomes attainable, paving the way to a relieving sense of accomplishment.

4. **Relief Algorithm Reflection:** Reflecting on how you naturally seek relief in daily life can be enlightening. Consider the habits or activities that offer you solace, and consciously integrate those practices more frequently into your routine for a consistently balanced state of mind.

5. **Visualization:** Visualization techniques are powerful tools for evoking a sense of relief. By mentally constructing scenarios where your stressors are resolved, you're able to experience and rehearse relief, reinforcing its positive effects and making it more accessible in times of need.

Incorporating these practices into your life allows for a healthier response to stress, promoting well-being and emotional recovery.

By the end of Chapter 24, you have discovered relief's role in emotional health and a repertoire of techniques to help you access this comforting state. As you embrace relief as an essential part of the cycle of stress and recovery, recognize it as a necessary emotion that brings balance and perspective to your life. This chapter celebrates relief as a vital component of emotional well-being and personal growth.

25

Romance

Romance, with its blend of affection, attraction, and passion, often carries with it a sense of whimsy and adventure, yet it also holds a deeper seriousness as it bonds individuals in a shared narrative. In this chapter, we delve into the complex nature of romance, examining how it plays a significant role in our lives and relationships. You can find insights and activities to nurture romance, whether it's a fleeting moment of connection or a lifelong love story.

THE WHIMSY AND SERIOUSNESS OF ROMANCE

Romance can be found in grand gestures and quiet moments alike, in the thrill of new love and the comfort of long-standing relationships. It's about creating shared experiences and deepening connections. Readers will meet characters like Isla, a novelist whose understanding of romance transcends the pages of her books to find expression in her own life, and James, whose weekly tradition of writing love notes to his partner keeps their romance alive through the ups and downs of daily life.

ISLA

In the quaint town of Seabreeze Haven, where tales of the heart wove seamlessly into the fabric of daily life, Isla found her muse among the whispers of the ocean and the rustle of turning pages. A novelist by trade and a dreamer at heart, Isla's books were windows to worlds of fervent romance and grandiose love. But beyond the ink and paper, her own life blossomed with the very essence of the love stories she penned.

Isla's days were draped in the solitude necessary for her craft, but her heart yearned for the companionship she so vividly depicted. She believed in a romance that was tangible, one that could be felt in the soft caress of the breeze or the gentle touch of the sun's warmth. Her belief was that romance should not be confined to fiction, but rather it should be a lived experience, rich and vibrant in its truth.

It was during one of her regular strolls along the beach, as she watched couples meandering along the shoreline, that Isla became aware of the depth of connection possible between two people. She longed for that connection, and it was this longing that bled into her stories, giving them a pulse.

Then, one summer evening, as the sun dipped into the embrace of the ocean, Isla's path intersected with Eli, a painter whose art captured the intangible beauty of Seabreeze Haven. Their encounter was serendipitous, a stroke of fate that Isla had often written about but never quite expected to live. Conversations flowed like the wine they shared, rich and intoxicating, and soon, their solo journeys merged into a shared expedition.

Romance, for Isla, was no longer just the dance of fictional characters but a dance she partook in with Eli. He showed her that gestures of love were not necessarily grandiose but found in the everyday attentiveness, in the easel he set up for her to write outdoors, or in the way her coffee was always ready when she woke, just the way she liked it.

The passion and ardor that Isla wrote about were mirrored in her real-life romance with Eli. Each moment with him was a chapter from her novels come to life, each glance a verse, each kiss a period at the end of a beautifully written sentence.

In the end, Isla's story was one of life imitating art. Her understanding of romance, so eloquently depicted through the narratives of her creation, found its echo in her reality with Eli. Together, they lived a romance that was not just read but experienced, a testament to the power of love to transcend the boundaries of fiction and bloom in the heart of one's own life.

JAMES

In the small, bustling town of Seabreeze Haven, where each sunrise painted the sky with promises and every sunset bid the day a colorful farewell, James cultivated a garden of affection not with flowers or sweet nothings, but with words etched on paper. A carpenter by trade, his hands were more accustomed to the roughness of wood than the smooth surface of paper, yet every Sunday morning, he laid down his tools to pick up a pen.

The love notes began as a single slip of paper tucked into the pocket of his partner's coat, a few hastily scribbled words that held within them the depth of his feelings. It was a simple act, one that carried the timbre of his voice and the touch of his hand in each letter that curved and straightened under his careful script.

As the tradition continued, these notes became the story of their life together. Each piece of paper held laughter, shared secrets, and the quiet confessions of a man whose heart was tethered to another. The notes chronicled their journey through the ordinary days that, when woven together, created the extraordinary fabric of their shared life.

Through times of joy, the notes sang of gratitude and wonder. When clouds gathered, the words became a beacon of hope, a reminder that after every storm, the sun was certain to shine. During the mundane rhythms of routine, the notes whispered of magic in the monotony, a charm that only two hearts in harmony could decipher.

James's partner found these tokens in unexpected places—the sugar jar, nestled between socks in a drawer, within the pages of a book—and with each discovery, the romance was rekindled. The notes were a weekly pause, a reminder to stop and cherish the love that grew and flourished in the most unassuming of soils.

As years unfurled, the collection of notes swelled, each one illustrating the resilience of their love. They were proof that romance need not be grand gestures or dramatic declarations. Instead, it could be found in the steady dedication of a man who, every week, chose to write his heart onto paper, crafting a romance that endured, one note at a time.

In Seabreeze Haven, James and his partner became known not for the life they led in public, but for the love they nurtured in the quiet corners of their world, a love that was as constant as the tide and as unique as the notes that captured it.

VISUALIZATION EXERCISES

Visualization Exercise 1: The Envelope of Love

Find a relaxing place to sit or lie down, and close your eyes. Breathe in deeply and, as you exhale, visualize yourself seated at a vintage writing desk, bathed in the golden glow of a candle. Before you is a stack of fine paper and a fountain pen filled with ink. This is your space to compose a love letter. Imagine dipping the pen into the ink and writing down your deepest affections, your gratitude, and your commitment to someone you love deeply. With each word, feel the warmth that comes from expressing your heart. Once the letter is complete, picture sealing it in an envelope and imagine the joy on your loved one's face as they receive it. Hold on to the warmth that this act of love has ignited in your heart.

Visualization Exercise 2: The Dance of Connection

Begin by focusing on your breath, feeling each inhale and exhale guiding you into a deeper state of relaxation. In your mind's eye, picture yourself in an elegant ballroom filled with soft music. You are dressed in your finest attire. As the music swells, you see your partner approaching. Take their hand and feel the connection as you begin to dance. With each step and turn, feel the romance in the air, the love that you share, and the harmony of your movements together. As the music continues, let this dance symbolize the journey of your relationship—the steps you've taken together, the rhythm you've found, and the love that leads you both.

Visualization Exercise 3: The Shared Sunset

Imagine yourself walking hand in hand with your partner on a deserted beach. The sky is ablaze with the fiery hues of the setting sun, and the gentle lapping of the waves accompanies your stroll. With each step on the soft sand, feel the sense of peace and romance that this serene setting brings. As the sun dips lower, find a place to sit together, shoulders touching, watching the spectacle of color. In this shared experience, feel the love and appreciation for the presence of your partner, for the moments of quiet intimacy, and for the beauty that surrounds you both. Hold this image and the feelings it evokes, letting it fill you with a sense of romantic connection. When you are ready, bring your awareness back to the present, carrying with you the emotions and tranquility from this visualization.

NURTURING ROMANCE IN LIFE

1. **Romantic Rituals:** Make it a priority to establish small rituals with your partner that create intimacy. Regularly scheduling moments like date nights or a shared morning routine can act as strong pillars in your relationship, keeping the spark alive.

2. **Appreciation and Affirmation:** Never underestimate the power of expressing appreciation. A simple "thank you" or heartfelt compliment can significantly bolster your bond. Try setting aside time each day to share something you value about each other.

3. **Adventurous Experiences:** Introducing elements of surprise or adventure can reignite the initial thrill you felt at the start of your relationship. Be open to trying new activities together, whether it's a cooking class or a spontaneous road trip.

4. **Mindful Listening:** Truly listening to your partner—with attention and without judgment—is one of the most loving acts in a relationship. Practice mindful listening to understand not just the words, but the feelings behind them.

5. **Romance Algorithm Reflection:** Take some time to reflect on your current romantic habits. What patterns do you notice? Are there areas you'd like to improve or change? Reflecting on these questions can help you make more conscious choices that align with your desires for romance.

By integrating these practices into your relationship, you not only nurture your bond but also create a shared journey that's rich with affection, understanding, and excitement.

As you turn the final page of Chapter 25, you have reconnected with both the joyous and serious aspects of romance and gained tools to incorporate its magic into your life. You will be reminded that romance is not just found in extraordinary events but also in the everyday efforts to show love, care, and interest. This chapter champions the idea that romance is a dynamic and evolving narrative, one that enriches life and brings color to your most cherished relationships.

26

Sadness

Sadness is an emotion that tugs at the heartstrings, often eliciting empathy, introspection, and a deep sense of humanity. In Chapter 26, we explore sadness not just as an emotion to be avoided but as a potential pathway to personal growth and understanding. This chapter offers compassionate insights into embracing sadness, along with strategies for transforming it into a constructive force in our lives.

SADNESS AS A PATHWAY TO GROWTH

Acknowledging sadness can lead to a deeper understanding of what matters most to us. It can act as a catalyst for change, pushing us to re-evaluate our lives and prioritize our happiness. Readers will be introduced to characters like Liam, who finds within his sadness a wellspring of creativity, and Rachel, whose grief leads to founding a community support group, turning her personal loss into communal healing.

LIAM

In a corner of Seabreeze Haven where the willow trees wept into the babbling brook, Liam discovered the paradoxical beauty of sadness. A writer whose soul was as deep and tumultuous as the ocean, he found his muse in the melancholy that often enveloped him like the town's characteristic morning fog.

Liam's relationship with sadness was complex. It was both a shroud that dulled the colors of the world and the lens that brought into focus the truths of the human experience. Where others found despair, Liam unearthed a strange kind of inspiration; a call to venture into the recesses of his heart and draw out words that resonated with the raw authenticity of feeling.

His creativity bloomed in the quiet hours of introspection, where the echoes of lost loves and bygone days danced with his thoughts. The tap of the keyboard became the rhythm of his catharsis, as stories poured forth, tinged with the bittersweet hues of his inner turmoil.

Liam's tales were not of grand victories or joyful reunions. They were intimate portraits of longing, of the quiet bravery in facing the day, of finding beauty in the breakdown. His characters were sculpted from the clay of his own vulnerabilities, resonating with readers who found solace in knowing their private sorrows were shared by another.

The books that lined the shelves of the local bookstore, each spine bearing Liam's name, were more than narratives; they were lifelines to those adrift in their own sea of sadness. They were proof that from the depths of despair could rise the most beautiful creations, that sadness was not an end but a beginning.

As Liam translated his personal melancholy into compelling narratives, he embraced the creativity that flowed from his sadness. His heartache became his art, and through his words, he found a way to express his own pain but also to transmute it into something timeless, something that spoke of the resilience and complexity of the human spirit.

In the embrace of his sadness, Liam found a purpose that transcended his own story, connecting the threads of his experience with the universal fabric of emotion. His creativity became his alchemy, turning the leaden weight of sorrow into the gold of artistic legacy.

RACHEL

In Seabreeze Haven, where every ebb and flow of the tide whispered of beginnings and endings, Rachel's story unfolded, one of loss and collective solace. Rachel, whose heart had known the sharp sting of grief, transformed her sorrow into a ray of hope for others. Through her pain, she became an architect of healing, constructing a haven for shared humanity within the community.

Rachel's journey through the valley of shadows began with the loss that shook her world—a tapestry torn, leaving threads frayed and loose. The absence she grappled with was profound, and in the silence of her loss, she sought the echo of other voices that understood the language of heartache.

With the resilience that often sprouts from the cracks of a broken heart, Rachel founded a support group, a gathering of souls seeking to mend the rent fabric of their lives. She named it "Harbor of Hope," a place where the grieving could dock their battered vessels, finding refuge in the storm of their emotions.

The group met weekly in the warmth of the community center, circled by the comfort of aged pines that stood sentinel outside. Each meeting began with Rachel's story, a tale not of defeat but of survival. Her narrative was a lighthouse, guiding others through the fog of their own sorrow.

In that space of shared experience, personal loss transcended into communal healing. Rachel's grief, once a chasm that threatened to swallow her whole, became the foundation upon which others could stand and gaze toward the horizon of their recovery.

Together, they shared memories, not to cling to the past, but to celebrate the lives that continued to shape their own. They learned to navigate the treacherous waters of grief, not as solitary wanderers but as a fleet united by their shared humanity and fortified by empathy.

As time passed, Harbor of Hope flourished. New members joined, each a unique stitch in the ever-expanding quilt of the support group. Rachel witnessed the transformation of her pain into a legacy of healing, her loss into a shared journey toward acceptance and peace.

In Seabreeze Haven, Harbor of Hope became a lasting organization, a reminder that even in the depths of despair, the human spirit can find a way to forge connections, to heal, and to emerge not unscarred but stronger in the broken places.

VISUALIZATION EXERCISES

Visualization Exercise 1: The Comforting Tree

Close your eyes and picture yourself walking in a serene forest. The air is crisp and filled with the scent of pine. As you walk, you come across a majestic tree with wide, welcoming branches. Under this tree, you feel safe enough to let your sadness surface. Visualize your sadness as leaves falling gently to the ground. With each leaf that falls, feel your burden lightening. The tree understands and absorbs your pain, offering you comfort. Sit with this tree, feel its ancient wisdom, and allow it to remind you that just like the seasons, your sadness will pass, and new growth will find its way through. When you feel ready, thank the tree and slowly bring your attention back to your surroundings, carrying with you a sense of release and peace.

Visualization Exercise 2: The River of Tears

Imagine yourself sitting by a gentle river in a quiet, beautiful place. Each drop of water in the river represents a tear of sadness. See yourself cupping the water in your hands and watching it overflow and trickle back into the river. Recognize that like the river, your tears are not a sign of weakness but a natural response to your emotions. They are part of a vast river of shared human experience. As you watch the river flow, acknowledge and honor your sadness, but also see it moving on, reminding you that your emotions are fluid and will change and evolve over time. Take a deep breath, and as you exhale, let go of a little bit of your sadness into the river. When you feel lighter, gently open your eyes.

Visualization Exercise 3: Letting Go at Sunrise

Imagine yourself standing on a quiet beach at sunrise. The sand is cool beneath your feet, and the gentle waves lap against the shore. In your hands, you hold a smooth, heavy stone that represents your sadness. As you take a deep breath, feel the weight of the stone. When you are ready, walk to the water's edge and, with intention, release the stone into the sea. Watch as it sinks beneath the waves, carried away by the tide. As the sun rises higher in the sky, feel the warmth on your skin and the lightness in your heart, knowing your sadness is being washed away, leaving space for peace and new beginnings.

EMBRACING AND TRANSFORMING SADNESS

1. **Mindful Acceptance:** Acknowledge your feelings of sadness without harsh self-criticism. Understand that sadness is a natural emotional response that merits attention and care. Allow yourself to feel without pushing your emotions away.
2. **Expressive Writing:** Use writing as a means to express your sadness. This could be through journaling, poetry, or letter writing. It's not only cathartic but also helps in making sense of your emotions.
3. **Art and Music:** Channel your sadness into creativity. Art and music can be powerful modes of expression, providing comfort and a way to communicate what might be hard to express with words alone.

4. **Physical Activity:** Engage in gentle physical activity like yoga, which can soothe both body and mind, or take walks to clear your thoughts and gain a new perspective.

5. **Social Support:** Reach out to friends, family, or support groups. Sharing your experiences with others can lighten the burden of sadness and remind you that you're not alone.

6. **Sadness Algorithm Reflection:** Reflect on how you typically respond to sadness. Do you allow yourself to fully experience it, or do you tend to suppress it? Understanding your patterns can help you develop healthier ways to cope with sadness when it arises.

Remember, allowing yourself to experience and express sadness is an integral part of the human experience, and it can lead to a richer, more authentic life.

As you conclude Chapter 26, you are building an understanding of the multifaceted role sadness plays in our lives. You have learned methods to engage with sadness constructively, viewing it not as an impediment but as an opportunity for emotional enrichment and growth. This chapter helps you to understand that sadness, when embraced and explored, can lead to greater empathy, creativity, and a renewed appreciation for the joys of life.

27

Satisfaction

Satisfaction is the fulfilling feeling that comes from achievement or the realization of one's desires and goals. It's a sense of completion, contentment, and often, a sign of progress. In Chapter 27, we examine the fulfilling nature of satisfaction and its vital role in motivating us toward our aspirations. This chapter provides guidance on setting meaningful goals and the importance of recognizing and celebrating our achievements.

THE FULFILLMENT OF SATISFACTION

Satisfaction can stem from various sources, whether it's completing a challenging project, making a meaningful contribution, or simply enjoying a job well done. It reinforces our actions and decisions, affirming that the effort we've invested has been worthwhile. Through characters like Charlotte who reaches her goal of running a marathon after months of training, and Jackson, who sees his community garden project come to fruition, we see how satisfaction acts as a marker of personal growth and communal contribution.

CHARLOTTE

In the serene town of Seabreeze Haven, where the waves echoed the town's heartbeat, Charlotte had set herself a monumental goal. Running a marathon was more than a test of physical endurance; it was a challenge she laid out to conquer her doubts and fears, to step beyond the ordinary into a realm of extraordinary personal achievement.

Sofia's training began as winter relinquished its hold to the budding promises of spring. Each morning, as the sun whispered its first rays over the horizon, her sneakers would thud against the cobblestone streets of the sleeping town.

Her breaths were rhythmic and determined, each one propelling her forward, each stride a victory over the voice that once told her she couldn't.

The months rolled by, and with them, Charlotte's strength grew. The long stretches of road that once daunted her now called out as old friends, each curve and hill a part of her story. She ran through rain that made her feel reborn, through wind that tested her resolve, under sunsets that painted her path in hues of triumph.

The marathon day arrived, a culmination of all the early mornings and aching muscles, of the commitment that tasted of both salt and sweetness. As Charlotte stood at the starting line, her heart was a drumline echoing with anticipation, and when the signal sounded, she surged forward with the tide of runners, a stream of dreams in motion.

The miles unfolded beneath her, marked by pain, elation, and relentless will. When the wall of fatigue hit, she scaled it with thoughts of each morning that had led her here, with the chorus of cheers that grew louder as she neared the finish line.

Crossing that line, Charlotte's arms raised in a victory that was hers alone to claim. The satisfaction that flooded her was as vast as the ocean that cradled Seabreeze Haven. It was the satisfaction of knowing she was capable of the incredible, of transforming the whispered "I wish" of yesterday into the shouted "I did" of today.

The satisfaction Sofia found in her marathon endeavor was about more than the medal placed around her neck; it was about the knowledge that she had pushed through her limitations, redefining her own boundaries. In her pursuit, she had not just run a marathon. She had traveled to the deepest parts of her spirit and found there an unyielding strength.

Back in Seabreeze Haven, Charlotte's story became a reminder that satisfaction lies not at the finish line, but in the courage to start and the resolve to keep moving forward, one step at a time.

JACKSON

Jackson, whose hands were more often found covered in soil than not, had long dreamt of a garden that would be the heart of Seabreeze Haven—a place where the community could come together, hands in the earth, cultivating not just plants but relationships and well-being.

The lot on Elm Street had stood empty and forgotten for years. Where others saw a barren plot, Jackson saw potential—a canvas awaiting a transformation. So, with a vision fueled by passion and a touch of green-fingered magic, he set forth to turn the soil of that lot into a thriving community garden.

It began with proposals and presentations to the town council, each meeting a step closer to his goal. Once permission was granted, Jackson's weekends were no longer his own. They belonged to the garden and, by extension, to the people of Seabreeze Haven.

Slowly, the empty lot began to change. Beds were raised, seeds were sown, and Jackson's dream started to take root. He worked tirelessly, his sweat mingling with the earth, his determination as steadfast as the sun. The project was a mosaic of challenges and victories, of early disappointments and blossoming successes.

When the first green shoots broke through the soil, it was more than the birth of plants; it was the germination of community spirit. People who once just nodded in passing now gathered to share stories over shared labor. Each tomato, every squash, every flower that bloomed was the fruit of the town's collective effort.

The day the garden officially opened was one of celebration. The people of Seabreeze Haven walked paths lined with lavender and rosemary, their senses caressed by the fragrance. Children's laughter mingled with the buzzing of bees, and in the midst of it all was Jackson, a quiet smile gracing his face.

The satisfaction Jackson felt was not merely because the garden thrived, but because it had become a living symbol of unity and hope. The garden was his legacy, but the joy it brought and the community it nurtured were the true fruits of his labor.

In the end, Jackson's satisfaction lay not in the act of planting, but in watching others reap the joy of the harvest. His personal growth was intertwined with the growth of each plant and the blooming of the community around it. The garden became a mirror reflecting the vibrant life of Seabreeze Haven, with Jackson at its genesis—a living example of what it means to cultivate not just the land, but the soul of a community.

VISUALIZATION EXERCISES

Visualization Exercise 1: The Garden of Accomplishment

Close your eyes and imagine yourself standing in the middle of a lush garden under a sky painted with the soft light of dusk. This is no ordinary garden—each plant and flower represents a goal you've accomplished or a challenge you've overcome. Walk along the stone path and pause to admire each one, touching the petals and leaves, feeling a sense of pride and contentment with every texture against your skin. The fragrances mix with the evening air, a sweet reminder of your journey. Sit on a bench and look around at this space you've cultivated with your efforts. Absorb the satisfaction that envelops you, knowing that each bloom speaks of your hard work and perseverance.

Visualization Exercise 2: The Tree of Growth

Begin by taking a deep breath, and as you exhale, envision a sapling sprouting from fertile ground. With every breath you take, the sapling grows, stronger and more vibrant. This tree is a symbol of your personal growth, each branch representing different aspects of your life where you have found satisfaction: career, personal relationships, self-improvement. See the tree flourish, its leaves rustling with the energy of your achievements. Climbing up to the highest branch, you gaze out to see the horizon—a vision of future goals and dreams yet to be realized, waiting just for you.

Visualization Exercise 3: The Mosaic of Memories

Picture yourself in a quiet room with walls adorned with mosaic tiles. Each tile is a vivid memory of a satisfying moment in your life—a kind word you said, a task completed, or a moment of simple pleasure. As you look at each tile, the scenes come to life, replaying those satisfying moments. Feel the warmth spread through you as you relive them. You're surrounded by the beauty of your own making, a life mosaic that is both unique and vibrant. With each memory, feel the swell of satisfaction grow within you, affirming that your life is full of accomplishments to be celebrated.

SETTING GOALS AND CELEBRATING ACHIEVEMENTS

1. **Goal-Setting Exercise:** Start by setting clear, attainable goals. Break them down into actionable steps and celebrate each milestone. This clarity can transform your aspirations into a tangible pathway to satisfaction.

2. **Mindful Reflection:** Make it a habit to pause each day to reflect on what went well. Notice even the smallest wins or moments of contentment. This mindfulness can amplify feelings of satisfaction that might otherwise go unnoticed.

3. **Achievement Rituals:** Establish your own rituals to celebrate successes. Whether it's a simple treat or a moment of silence, honoring your achievements can solidify the rewarding feeling of accomplishment.

4. **Gratitude Practices:** Regularly express gratitude, either privately in a journal or directly to those who support you. Recognizing others' roles in your success can deepen relationships and multiply the joys of your achievements.

5. **Satisfaction Algorithm Reflection:** Reflect on the occurrences that bring you the most satisfaction. Are they related to personal achievements, connections with others, or overcoming challenges? Identifying these can help you seek out and create more such fulfilling experiences.

By embracing these practices, you can build a more satisfying life, marked by appreciation for the journey as well as the destination.

You are deepening your connection to satisfaction and building strategies to unlock the use of this emotion in your personal and professional life. You can set and achieve goals that bring satisfaction and acknowledge your progress along the way. This chapter highlights satisfaction as an emotional reward for your efforts, a necessary component for a balanced and fulfilling life.

28

Sexual Desire

Sexual desire is a natural and integral part of the human experience, encompassing a spectrum of feelings that can be powerful and, at times, complex to manage. In the chapter that follows, we approach sexual desire with sensitivity and openness, exploring its role in personal and interpersonal dynamics. This chapter offers guidance on understanding sexual desire, its healthy expression, and the importance of clear and respectful communication.

NAVIGATING THE COMPLEXITIES OF SEXUAL DESIRE

Sexual desire can be influenced by biological, psychological, and social factors, and can vary greatly among individuals. Recognizing and respecting this diversity is crucial for a healthy relationship with our own desires and in our interactions with others. Through the stories of individuals like Gemini, who is learning to balance his desires within his relationship, and Capricorn, who is discovering what desire means for her personally, we'll explore the multifaceted nature of sexual desire.

GEMINI

In the rhythm of Seabreeze Haven's ebbing tides, Gemini was finding his way through the intricate dance of intimacy and connection. He had begun a relationship rich with affection and mutual respect, but navigating a newfound sexual desire presented a challenge—a delicate balancing act between personal longing and shared harmony.

Gemini's exploration into the realm of desire was not just a pursuit of pleasure but, a deeper quest to understand the language of love in its most physical form. It was about learning to express his needs while tuning into the subtle whispers of his partner's wishes, finding a common tempo that resonated with both their hearts.

Their communication became a bridge over which their truest feelings could pass without fear or reservation. Open conversations held in the sanctuary of their shared space allowed vulnerability to become the cornerstone of trust, and from this foundation, their sexual connection deepened.

It was in the giving that Gemini discovered the joy of reciprocity, in the quiet inquiry into his partner's eyes where he found the reflection of his own desires acknowledged and embraced. Each encounter was a step toward understanding, each moment of closeness, a lesson in the art of giving and receiving.

In the intimacy they shared, Gemini found his desires were not a singular drive but a mutual experience that continued to strengthen their relationship. The balance he sought and found was not a static point but a fluid harmony that moved with them through the seasons of their love.

As Gemini and his partner continued to explore the depths of their desires together, their bond transcended the physical. The connection that sparked in the dim light of their bedroom ignited a flame that illuminated all aspects of their union.

The story of Gemini's gradual understanding of his own sexual desire shows us the importance of balance in the most intimate of human connections. It was a dance that, when performed with care, respect, and open heartedness, could elevate the act of love into a form of communication beyond words, where each could meet the other in the perfect silence of shared satisfaction.

CAPRICORN

Capricorn's tale began at a crossroads of self-discovery, nestled in the heart of Seabreeze Haven, where every whispering wave seemed to echo her quest for understanding. She embarked on a journey not outward but inward, uncovering the layers of her own sexuality and desire, seeking to unearth and embrace the full spectrum of her identity.

For Capricorn, desire was not a simple thread but a complex weave of emotions, thoughts, and physicality. She sought to unravel this mystery, to understand the patterns woven by her past experiences, her personal values, and the innate calls of her body.

Her journey was both solitary and shared. With trusted friends and in the sanctity of support groups, she voiced her questions and uncertainties, finding solace in shared experiences. Through books and the canvas of her own journal, she charted the land-scapes of her desires, each page bringing her closer to clarity.

As Capricorn explored, she discovered that her desires were not fixed stars but constellations that changed shape with time. They were influenced by the intimate connections she fostered, by the gentle touch of her partner Gemini, by the rush of an en-counter that left her both grounded and afloat.

Sexual desire, for Capricorn was not just a quest for pleasure but a deeper yearning for connection—physical, yes, but also emo-tional and intellectual. It was a yearning for someone who could meet her on all these levels, who could dance with her through the ebb and flow of intimacy with a harmony that resonated to the core.

In her own embrace, she found the power of self-love, recog-nizing that before she could share her desires with another, she needed to understand and accept them herself. This realization was a breakthrough, a moment where the light of comprehension dawned, clear and bright.

Capricorn learned that her sexuality was her own—unique and valid. It was a river that ran its course through the landscape of her being, feeding into the ocean of who she was. She learned that desire could be a whisper as much as a roar, a solitary spark as well as a shared flame.

In Seabreeze Haven, Capricorn began a one-woman odyssey to chart the waters of desire and emerge with a map that was hers alone. Her voyage through the multifaceted nature of sexual desire illuminated a path for others of self-exploration, acceptance, and the infinite possibilities that come with truly knowing oneself.

VISUALIZATION EXERCISES

Visualization Exercise 1: The Flame of Connection

Picture yourself in a peaceful room where a single candle burns on a table. This flame represents your sexual desire, a natural and integral part of who you are. As you focus on the flame, see it flicker and dance, its warmth and light filling the space. Visualize the flame growing larger as you acknowledge and embrace your desires, allowing them to expand without judgment. Feel the warmth envelop you, representing a loving and positive connection with yourself. As the flame burns steadily, imagine it also represents the warmth and connection you can share with a partner, one that respects both your needs and boundaries. Let this visualization affirm that your sexual desires are healthy and can lead to deep connections.

Visualization Exercise 2: The Blossoming Garden

Close your eyes and envision yourself walking through a vibrant garden, alive with the colors of lush flowers in full bloom. Each flower represents a facet of your sexual desire, beautiful and unique. As you walk, notice how some flowers attract you more than others—these are the aspects of your desire that resonate with you deeply. Take time to admire these flowers, allowing yourself to experience their beauty without shame or hesitation. Feel a sense of gratitude for this natural part of yourself as you accept and appreciate the diversity of your desires, understanding that they contribute to the rich garden of your being.

Visualization Exercise 3: The Ocean's Tide

Imagine standing at the shore of a vast ocean at sunset, the waves gently lapping at your feet. Each wave that reaches you is like a pulse of your sexual desire, strong and full of life. Breathe deeply, and with each inhale, draw in the energy of the ocean. With each exhale, release any inhibitions or fears back to the sea. Visualize the tide as the ebb and flow of your own desires, sometimes calm, and at other times, more intense. Acknowledge this natural rhythm, accepting it as part of your life's flow. Allow yourself to feel connected to this power, knowing you can ride the waves of desire with confidence and self-assurance.

HEALTHY EXPRESSION AND COMMUNICATION

1. **Sexual Desire Reflection:** Take time to reflect on what sparks your desire. Understanding the "why" behind your attraction can offer insights into your personal patterns and preferences.
2. **Open Dialogue:** Engage in transparent conversations with your partner about your desires. Use clear communication to establish consent and mutual respect, ensuring that both partners feel heard and valued.
3. **Boundary Setting:** Learn to articulate and respect your own boundaries and those of your partner. Healthy relationships are built on the foundation of mutual understanding about what each person is comfortable with.

4. **Educational Resources:** Educate yourself on sexual health and desire through credible sources. A well-informed understanding can enhance your experience and debunk common misconceptions, leading to a healthier sexual life.

5. **Emotional Intelligence:** Work on developing a keen sense of emotional intelligence regarding sexual desire. Recognize and respond to your own emotions and those of your partner, which can deepen your connection and enrich your shared experiences.

By integrating these practices into your life, you can cultivate a fulfilling and compassionate approach to sexual desire that honors both your needs and those of your partner.

As you conclude this chapter, you are learning to connect with your sexual desire and assembling the tools for its healthy expression and communication. The aim is to equip you with the knowledge and confidence to fulfill your desires responsibly and joyfully, contributing to satisfying and respectful relationships. We can see sexual desire as a natural part of human life, one to be understood and celebrated with care and consideration.

29

Surprise

Surprise is the jolt of the unexpected, a sudden disruption of the anticipated that can evoke delight or dismay. In Chapter 29, we explore the dynamics of surprise, recognizing its potential to energize and its power to unsettle. This chapter is about embracing the unexpected, learning to respond to surprises with grace and finding the opportunities they often bring.

THE DELIGHT AND DISMAY OF SURPRISE

Surprise can shake us out of complacency, spark innovation, or cause discomfort when it challenges our sense of control. We'll examine the dual nature of surprise through the experiences of characters like Ava, who receives an unexpected promotion, and Tom, whose surprise at a sudden life change leads him on a path of self-discovery. Through their stories, we learn that surprise, whether delightful or dismaying, is a natural part of the ebb and flow of life.

AVA

Ava's career at the Seabreeze Haven library had been a steady climb, each step a result of her dedication and love for literature. She had become as much a part of the library as the timeless volumes that lined its shelves. Yet, for all her hard work, Ava never sought recognition; she found fulfillment in the quiet thanks of patrons and the hush of the reading rooms.

One ordinary Tuesday, as she was re-shelving a collection of maritime tales, the library director, Mr. Penrose, called her into his office. Ava walked in, her mind adrift with thoughts of overdue book reports and the evening's storytelling session for children.

What Mr. Penrose offered, however, was a narrative twist Ava could not have foreseen. "Ava," he began, with a gravity that belied his usual jovial tone, "your service to this institution has been the quiet force behind our success. It's time that force was recognized." He slid an envelope across the desk, and with a smile that crinkled the corners of his eyes, he continued, "Congratulations. You're going to be our new Head Librarian."

The words took a moment to register. A promotion? Her? Ava's heart fluttered like the pages of a book caught in the breeze. A rush of emotions cascaded through her—astonishment, disbelief, and a burgeoning joy that bloomed like the town's spring azaleas.

In the days that followed, Ava moved through her familiar haunts of the library, her new title both a badge of honor and a cloak of surprise that she wore with humble pride. Her colleagues celebrated her, patrons smiled wider, and the books seemed to stand a little taller on their shelves.

The surprise promotion brought about a realization in Ava, a recognition of her own worth and the impact she had on the people who passed through the library's grand oak doors. It also awakened her to the delightful unpredictability of life, where sometimes the most extraordinary moments come wrapped in the guise of an ordinary day.

In this chapter of her life, Ava found that surprise could be a beautiful serendipity, a reminder that the world is full of hidden chapters waiting to be discovered, and that sometimes, those chapters have our names etched into their titles.

TOM

In Seabreeze Haven, where the unexpected is often hidden in the folds of the ocean mist, Tom's life was a series of well-planned events and predictable routines. He was a man of habit, finding comfort in the reassuring tick of the clock and the calendar squares neatly marked with daily tasks. That was until the day a surprise swept in like a gust of wind, flipping his world upside down and setting his compass spinning.

It was a Wednesday like any other when Tom received the news that his company was restructuring, and his role was being made redundant. The job he had known—the job that had defined his daily existence—was suddenly no more. In the hollow silence of his office, with the last echo of the announcement ringing in his ears, Tom felt the foundations of his world shift.

The surprise of this life change initially gripped Tom with a paralyzing fear, the kind that constricts breath and blurs vision. But as the initial shock subsided, a seed of something new began to sprout. Tom found himself standing at the threshold of the unknown, peering out with a mix of trepidation and a growing spark of excitement.

With time on his hands and a severance package in his pocket, Tom started on a journey of self-discovery. He revisited old dreams shelved in the attic of his mind, dusted off ambitions, and looked at them under the bright light of possibility. He took a road trip along the coast, each new town a chapter in his unfolding story, each new face a reflection of the varied chapters of humanity.

Tom learned to sail, the unpredictability of the sea a metaphor for life's own capricious nature. He volunteered, finding purpose in helping hands and shared stories. With every new experience, Tom's surprise at life's sudden twists softened into gratitude for the opportunity to rewrite his narrative.

The surprise that had once seemed like an end became a beginning. Tom's journey was not just about finding a new job or filling his days with activities; it was about rediscovering who he was when not confined by routine. It was about learning that sometimes, the most meaningful surprises are not the events themselves, but what we find within us when we rise to meet them.

VISUALIZATION EXERCISES

Visualization Exercise 1: The Unopened Door

Imagine yourself walking down a familiar hallway lined with doors. Each door represents an aspect of your life. You notice one door you've never seen before. It's intriguing, beckoning you closer. Place your hand on the doorknob, feel its texture and notice the sense of curiosity bubbling within you. As you open the door, a gentle light spills out, engulfing you in warmth. Step through the doorway and discover a room filled with treasures and possibilities you had never imagined. Allow yourself to feel the wonder and excitement of this surprise, acknowledging the new opportunities it brings.

Visualization Exercise 2: The Gift of the Unexpected

Close your eyes and envision yourself receiving a beautifully wrapped gift. The anticipation of what's inside fills you with a thrilling sense of mystery. Carefully, you unwrap the present, and with each fold of paper that falls away, you allow yourself to release preconceived notions and expectations. Inside, you find an object that symbolizes a delightful and wholly unexpected turn in your life's path. Hold this symbol in your hands, examine it, and embrace the joy of the unknown. Let this experience remind you that life's surprises can bring untold joys.

Visualization Exercise 3: The Turning of the Seasons

Visualize yourself sitting in a serene park, observing the changing seasons. As each season passes, you witness the landscape transform in surprising ways: blossoms in spring, a canopy of green in summer, vibrant autumn leaves, and the silent beauty of winter snow. As you watch these changes, think about the surprises in your own life and how they've shaped and transformed you over time. Reflect on the beauty of each surprise and how, like the seasons, they come with their own unique set of experiences and lessons that contribute to your growth.

EMBRACING THE UNEXPECTED

1. **Flexibility Training:** Engage in mental exercises like "what if" scenarios to enhance cognitive flexibility. The ability to pivot your thoughts and expectations allows you to manage life's surprises with greater ease.

2. **Mindfulness Practice:** Ground yourself in the present with mindfulness. Techniques such as focused breathing or meditation can prepare you to accept the unforeseen without undue stress.

3. **Scenario Planning:** Think ahead about potential scenarios, not to fret about what might happen, but to build confidence in your capacity to handle the unexpected. This planning isn't about having all the answers, but about knowing you can find them.

4. **Surprise Algorithm Reflection:** Reflect on past surprises, both pleasant and challenging. What did they teach you? How did you adapt? These reflections can shape your responses to future surprises.

5. **Cultivating Curiosity:** Embrace the unexpected as an opportunity for growth and discovery. When you approach life with curiosity, surprises become less about shock and more about the possibilities they present.

Incorporating these strategies into your routine can not only help you manage the initial jolt of surprise but can also help you appreciate the potential for growth and excitement that comes with the unknown.

As this chapter closes, the appreciation for the role of surprise in your life has grown and you have unlocked a set of tools to engage with the unexpected in positive ways. You understand that surprise is not something to be feared but rather an invitation to grow, learn, and experience life more fully. This chapter encourages you to see the potential in every surprise, turning the unforeseen into a welcome adventure in the journey of life.

30

Emotional Synthesis

In the final chapter, we synthesize our journey through the diverse landscape of emotions, integrating the learning from each chapter into a cohesive whole. This chapter is about forming an emotional algorithm, a personal blueprint that helps us navigate our emotional lives with understanding and intention.

INTEGRATING EMOTIONAL LEARNING

Emotional learning involves more than understanding each emotion in isolation; it's about seeing how they interact and influence each other and our overall well-being. We'll revisit key lessons from each chapter and discuss how to apply this knowledge in various contexts, recognizing patterns and building emotional intelligence.

As you sit on the familiar bench overlooking Seabreeze Haven, the tranquil sounds of the harbor lulling the evening into night, take a moment to reflect on your journey through the many emotions we've explored together.

1. **Admiration:** Think back to the chapter on admiration. Who in your life sparks this feeling, and how can recognizing this admiration guide your choices and relationships?

2. **Adoration:** Recall the stories of deep adoration. What or whom do you adore in such a way that it inspires you to act, to create, or to nurture growth in yourself and others?

3. **Aesthetic Appreciation:** When you considered aesthetic appreciation, what beauty in your everyday life did you discover that had previously gone unnoticed?

4. **Amusement:** How can the lightheartedness of amusement be a balm during challenging times? When was the last time you allowed yourself to revel in amusement?

5. **Anger:** Anger can be a difficult emotion. How can you use the energy of anger constructively to advocate for change or to protect your boundaries?

6. **Anxiety:** In times of anxiety, what grounding practices can you employ to return to a state of calm?

7. **Awe:** How can experiences of awe elevate your perspective on life and its mysteries?

8. **Awkwardness:** Can you embrace awkwardness as a sign of authenticity in your interactions, allowing it to lead to more genuine connections?

9. **Boredom:** When you feel boredom creeping in, what new exploration or creative endeavor could reignite your engagement with the world?

10. **Calmness:** In moments of turmoil, how can you find your center of calm, and what does this sanctuary look like for you?

11. **Confusion:** When faced with confusion, what steps can you take to clarify your thoughts and make decisions aligned with your true path?

12. **Craving:** How can you balance your cravings to ensure they contribute to your well-being rather than detract from it?

13. **Disgust:** What can your reactions of disgust teach you about your core values and boundaries?

14. **Empathic Pain:** How can empathic pain be acknowledged in a way that fosters compassion without overwhelming you?

15. **Entrancement:** What activities lead you to a state of entrancement, and how can this absorption enhance your life experience?

16. **Excitement:** What excites you about your future, and how can you channel this excitement to realize your aspirations?

17. **Fear:** Fear can be a protective signal or a barrier. How can you distinguish between the two to live courageously?

18. **Horror:** After witnessing or learning of something horrific, what strategies can you use to process and recover from this intense emotion?

19. **Interest:** In which areas would you like to deepen your interest, and how can you actively pursue this knowledge or skill?

20. **Joy:** What are the simplest sources of joy in your life, and how can you invite more of this pure joy into your daily routine?

21. **Love:** How does love manifest in your life, and in what ways can you express and cultivate this profound emotion?

22. **Nostalgia:** Reflect on the warm embrace of nostalgia. How can you honor these memories without letting them overshadow the present?

23. **Relief:** Consider a moment of relief you've experienced. How did you acknowledge and celebrate this turning point?

24. **Romance:** Whether with a partner or in life's passions, how does romance show up for you, and how can you nurture it?

25. **Sadness:** How can you honor your sadness as a necessary emotion that has the capacity to deepen your empathy and understanding?

26. **Satisfaction:** What recent achievement has given you satisfaction, and how can you build on this success?

27. **Sexual Desire:** In understanding your sexual desires, how can you ensure they enrich your life and relationships?

28. **Surprise:** How can you stay open and adaptable to the surprises life throws your way, finding the hidden gifts within them?

29. **Synthesis of Emotions:** Now, with these chapters as your guide, how can you synthesize your emotional experiences to create a personal algorithm that fosters a balanced, fulfilling life?

Your emotional algorithm is your unique blueprint for navigating life's complex emotional landscape. It's a living document, open to revisions and improvements as you grow and change. As you ponder these questions, know that you have the power to program and reprogram this algorithm, crafting a life rich with emotional wisdom and resilience.

31

Personal Blueprint

Emotional Mind Map

Choose Your Format: Decide whether you prefer a digital tool or paper for your mind map. Digital tools can be convenient and easily adjustable, but paper can offer a tactile, free-form experience without the distraction of technology.

Start with Emotions: Place an emotion that you frequently experience at the center of your map. This could be joy, anger, anxiety, or any other emotion you want to explore.

Branch Out with Triggers: From this central emotion, draw branches outward for different triggers. What specific events or interactions prompt this feeling? Be as detailed and specific as possible.

Detail Your Responses: For each trigger, create sub-branches to represent your typical responses. These could include your immediate reactions, coping mechanisms, or avoidance strategies.

Interactions and Consequences: Extend your map to include the outcomes of your emotional responses. How do they affect your interactions with others and your feelings about yourself?

Reflection and Patterns: Take a step back to review your map. Look for patterns. Do certain triggers consistently lead to unhelpful responses? Are there positive responses that you'd like to reinforce?

Plan for Change: Use your insights to create a plan for emotional growth. Choose one pattern you'd like to change and brainstorm alternative responses or coping strategies. Add these to your map.

Regular Updates: Treat your emotional mind map as a living document. As you learn more about your emotions and how they interact with your life, update and refine your map.

Remember, the goal is not to judge your emotions or responses but to understand them. This understanding can empower you to make more conscious choices about how you manage and express your feelings.

1. Personal Emotional Profiles

Creating a personal emotional profile is like drawing a map of your inner emotional landscape. It can help you navigate your feelings and behaviors, and understand how they fit into the broader context of your life. Here's how to create your own emotional profile, using the insights from the chapters of this book and the personalized algorithm score from the **Algorithm of You app:**

Review Emotion Chapters: Start by revisiting each chapter on emotions. For each emotion—joy, sadness, fear, disgust, etc.—take notes on what resonates with you. How do you typically experience these emotions, and what triggers them?

Analyze Your Algorithm Scores: Look at your personalized algorithm scores from the Algorithm of You app. How do these scores reflect your typical emotional responses and behaviors? Are there any surprises or insights that stand out?

Identify Patterns: Cross-reference the emotional chapters with your algorithm scores. Do you see any patterns emerging? Maybe you score high on joy but find that it's often triggered by external validation, or you might discover that your fear responses are more internal, linked to past experiences.

Catalog Emotions: Create a structured profile by listing each emotion and detailing how you experience it. Include your triggers, physiological responses, typical thoughts, and behaviors. Be as detailed as possible.

Behavioral Responses: For each emotion, write down how you usually respond. Do you confront it, explore it, or do you find ways to distract yourself? This is where you start building the framework for understanding your emotional behaviors.

Coping Mechanisms: Detail the coping mechanisms you currently use for each emotion. Are they healthy and effective? If not, what alternative strategies can you employ?

Personal Growth Goals: Using the information you've compiled, set specific goals for personal growth. For example, if you find that anxiety leads to avoidance behaviors, you might set a goal to practice mindfulness or confrontational exercises to build resilience.

Develop Emotional Habits: Consider how you can incorporate new emotional habits into your daily routine. Perhaps you start a gratitude journal to enhance joy or practice grounding exercises for moments of anxiety.

Ongoing Reflection: Regularly update your emotional profile. As you grow and change, your emotional experiences will too. Keep a journal or use the app to track these changes over time.

Share and Discuss: If you feel comfortable, discuss your profile with a trusted friend, family member, or therapist. Sharing can provide new insights and support as you work on your personal growth.

Remember, this is a deeply personal process. There's no right or wrong way to feel or respond to your emotions. The goal is self-understanding and growth, not self-judgment.

1. **Life Scenario Simulations:** To effectively apply your emotional learning to real-life situations, engaging in life scenario simulations can be a valuable exercise. These simulations are designed to prepare you for a variety of life events and interactions, providing a safe space to practice and refine your decision-making and interpersonal skills.

Here's a guide to help you set up and benefit from these simulations:

Select Scenarios: Choose scenarios that are relevant to your life or that you find challenging. This might be handling conflict at work, dealing with family dynamics, navigating social gatherings, or making tough personal decisions.

Define Objectives: For each scenario, clearly define what a successful outcome looks like for you. Is it to remain calm, to communicate effectively, to reach a compromise, or to assert your boundaries?

Simulate Realistically: Create a simulation as close to reality as possible. You can do this through role-playing exercises with a friend or by visualizing the scenario in detail. Use props or settings that add to the realism if necessary.

Apply Emotional Strategies: As you engage in the simulation, consciously apply the emotional strategies you've learned. Use techniques like deep breathing for calmness, affirmations for confidence, or perspective-taking to understand others' points of view.

Reflect on the Process: After each simulation, take the time to reflect. What did you learn? How did you feel? What worked well, and what could be improved? This reflection helps to consolidate learning and prepare you for real-life application.

Adjust Tactics: Based on your reflection, make adjustments to your approach. This might mean trying different communication techniques or altering how you manage your emotions in the moment.

Repeat and Practice: Repetition is key to mastering any skill. Regularly revisit these simulations, especially before anticipated life events that may be similar to your scenarios.

Seek Feedback: If possible, get feedback from others who participate in or observe the simulation. Constructive feedback can offer new insights and help you refine your approach.

Transfer to Real Life: Finally, take what you've practiced in simulations and apply it to real-life situations. Start with low-stakes environments and gradually work up to more challenging scenarios.

Remember, the goal of these simulations is not to prescribe a one-size-fits-all reaction but to provide a sandbox where you can explore different approaches and learn from them, ultimately enhancing your emotional agility and readiness for life's varied situations.

1. **Creating Your Emotional Algorithm:** As you navigate the landscape of your emotions, consider leveraging the tools and resources available through the Algorithm of You platform. Engage with our practitioners who specialize in mapping out emotional algorithms, guiding you through personalized strategies that resonate with your unique experiences.

Utilize our bespoke app that features an algorithm score—a reflective metric to help you monitor and understand your emotional tendencies. The app provides actionable insights and suggests exercises to improve your emotional agility.

Additionally, our online platform serves as a repository of knowledge and support, hosting a variety of workshops that delve into the intricacies of emotional algorithms. These sessions are designed to equip you with even more tools to better process and navigate your emotional world.

To deepen your understanding, explore our series of books, each one focusing on a facet of the emotional algorithm. These books complement the interactive elements of our app and workshops, providing a comprehensive framework for personal growth.

Keep in mind that your emotional algorithm is a dynamic journey, one that benefits from the synergy of expert guidance, interactive technology, and continued learning. Through the *Algorithm of You*, you are not just discovering an algorithm but also actively participating in its creation, ensuring it aligns with your evolving goals and experiences.

As we conclude this exploration of our own emotions, you are now equipped with a deep understanding of your own unique emotional algorithms that serve as a guide through the complexities of your emotional universe.

This synthesis of emotions empowers you to approach your feelings with wisdom, harnessing your emotions to live a richer, more fulfilling life. This final chapter reinforces the concept that emotions, when understood and integrated, can lead to profound personal transformation and a heightened sense of connection with yourself and the world.

32

Conclusion

THE EMOTIONAL LANDSCAPE: A JOURNEY OF DISCOVERY AND MASTERY

In the concluding chapter, we invite you to embark on the ultimate expedition across the vast terrain of your own emotional landscape. This is not a journey of miles, but of self-discovery and mastery. Here's how you can navigate this personal adventure:

Map Your Emotional Landscape: Begin by acknowledging the range of emotions you've encountered throughout this book. Sketch a mental map of your emotional experiences—where have you felt joy, stumbled into sadness, or discovered surprise? Recognize the paths you've taken and the emotional milestones you've reached.

Embrace the Terrain: Each emotion is a different terrain with its own features and challenges. Some emotions are like mountains that take effort to climb; others are like serene lakes that provide peace. Embrace the variety of these terrains, understanding that each contributes to the richness of your inner world.

Prepare for the Journey: Just as you would pack for a physical journey, gather tools for emotional mastery. These might include reflective practices like journaling, mindfulness techniques, or creative outlets. Equip yourself with patience, kindness, and the willingness to be vulnerable.

Set Forth with Intention: With your map and tools ready, set out with intention. Choose which emotional paths you want to explore further and which you may need to travel with care. Your intentions will serve as compass points, guiding your choices and interactions.

Learn the Art of Navigation: As you traverse your emotional landscape, learn the art of navigation. This means recognizing when to push forward through challenging emotions and when to rest and seek shelter in comfort. Cultivate resilience and adaptability to weather your emotional storms.

Celebrate the Viewpoints: Along your journey, there will be moments of breathtaking clarity and perspective. Celebrate these. Whether it's the summit of achievement or the quiet valley of reflection, take time to appreciate the view and how far you've come.

Share Your Journey: Just as landscapes are meant to be shared, so too are the stories of our emotional journeys. Share your experiences with others and listen to theirs. These shared stories deepen our understanding and connect us in our common humanity.

Keep Exploring: Remember, the emotional landscape is ever-changing. New paths will open as you grow and change. Stay curious and open to exploration, for it is through continuous discovery that we master our emotional selves.

As you integrate these principles into your life, you're not just reading a book; you're writing your own. Your emotional landscape is a living, breathing space where every step is a story, every challenge is a chapter, and every triumph is a milestone in your personal epic. Take the helm, dear reader, and steer your journey with courage and heart.

As the sun casts its last golden rays over the horizon of Seabreeze Haven, we close the pages of this chapter. Yet this is not an end, but a beginning. A beginning of a continuous cycle of growth, adaptation, and evolution of your emotions. This book has laid the groundwork, providing you with the algorithm concepts necessary to navigate your emotional world. Now it's time to take these lessons and apply them to the real-world complexities of decision-making and problem-solving.

CONTINUOUS GROWTH: ADAPTING AND EVOLVING WITH EMOTIONS

Your emotional algorithms are dynamic. As you face new situations and challenges, your understanding of your emotions and how they guide your decisions will evolve. Like any algorithm, they require updates and adjustments. Use this book as a living document—a reference to return to when you encounter new emotional puzzles. Ask yourself:

- How has my understanding of this emotion changed?
- What new strategies can I apply when this emotion arises?
- How can this emotion serve as a guide rather than a barrier?

FROM DISCOVERY TO MASTERY: THE SECOND BOOK

Your journey into the realm of emotions sets the stage for the next phase: understanding the type of problem-solving that resonates with you. The forthcoming book in this series will examine the ways your emotional responses influence your approach to problems. It's one thing to recognize and name an emotion, and another to understand how it fuels your problem-solving tactics.

Do you approach challenges with logic, tempered by empathy? Does anxiety motivate you to find meticulous solutions, or does excitement drive your creativity? The next book will offer a deeper exploration of these questions, helping you to develop a personal problem-solving algorithm that is as unique as your fingerprint.

THE ALGORITHM OF YOU: A GUIDED CONTINUATION

As you move forward, remember that you are the programmer of your life. The emotional algorithms you've discovered here are the codes that unlock your potential. Carry them into your daily life and let them guide you to tailor solutions that not only solve problems but also enhance your understanding of yourself.

Encourage yourself to:

- Reflect on the emotional responses that come naturally to you in problem-solving scenarios.
- Observe how these emotions influence your decisions, for better or worse.
- Refine your emotional algorithms as you gain insight, ensuring they align with your evolving goals and values.

Embrace the continuous loop of learning, adapting, and growing. The algorithm of you is not static; it's a living, breathing blueprint that shapes and is shaped by your experiences. This book has started you on the path. Now, step confidently into the journey ahead, equipped with the knowledge that your emotions are your allies in the art of problem-solving.

As you turn the final page, the invitation stands open: Continue this exploration with the next book and beyond. The algorithm of you awaits, ready to be discovered, understood, and mastered.

Stay Connected

Stay Connected

Thank you for joining us and choosing yourself on this journey through **Algorithm of You®**. We hope the insights and strategies shared here empower you to navigate life's challenges with confidence, resilience, and self-awareness. As you continue your path of growth, remember that this is just the beginning. We're here to support you every step of the way.

To stay connected and keep the momentum going, here are some ways you can join our community and access more resources:

◈ Visit Our Website: *www.algorithmofyou.com*

To explore more about the Algorithm of You® series, visit our website for personalized attunement services, webinars, classes, podcasts, live events, book signings, and transformational experiences.

Join our exclusive membership community for ongoing support, deeper insights, and connections with like-minded individuals. Engage in a space dedicated to growth, healing, and mastery, where you can access special events, exclusive content, and personalized guidance on your journey with *Algorithm of You®* .

◈ Follow Us on Social Media

Connect with us for daily inspiration, tips, and engaging discussions:

- **Instagram:** @you.decoded, @AOY.decoded, @raena.decoded

- **Facebook:** @you.decoded, @joshuastibal, @raenastibal

◈ Join Our Monthly Webinars

Dive deeper into topics like problem-solving, emotional intelligence, and personal growth. Sign up for our free monthly webinars, where we explore practical tools and answer your questions live.

◈ Check Out Our Other Books

Discover the full **Algorithm of You** series and continue your journey with us. Each book is designed to guide you in mastering different aspects of personal development and inner transformation.

Thank you for being a part of the *Algorithm of You®* community. We can't wait to see where this journey takes you. Remember, every step you take brings you closer to a more empowered and authentic you.

With love and gratitude,

Joshua & Raena Stibal

World Healers Inc.

Joshua Stibal is a thought leader in emotional intelligence, cognitive frameworks, and personal development. With a background in strategic thinking and algorithmic problem-solving, he brings a unique approach to understanding the intricate systems that drive human emotions. His work integrates logic and emotional awareness, helping individuals decode and optimize their emotional responses for personal and professional success. As a co-creator of *Algorithm of You®*, Joshua brings a unique perspective by blending analytical precision with deep self awareness, empowering people to navigate life with clarity and confidence. His passion for helping others uncover their inner potential has made him a sought-after mentor and educator in the fields of emotional mastery and self-improvement. He believes that by mastering emotional flow, individuals can unlock their full potential and move through life with greater purpose and harmony.

Raena Stibal is a transformational educator and mentor specializing in emotional well-being, personal growth, intuitive development, and self-discovery. With years of experience and a deep commitment to helping individuals recognize and harness their emotions, she provides guidance that fosters healing, empowerment, and clarity. Her work is rooted in holistic transformation, encouraging people to embrace their emotional experiences as a pathway to greater self-awareness and fulfillment. As a co-creator of *Algorithm of You®*, Raena brings a profound understanding of emotional patterns and their impact on human behavior. She blends intuitive insight with practical wisdom, offering tools to help individuals navigate their emotions with grace and resilience. Her compassionate and insightful approach has helped countless individuals redefine their relationships with themselves and the world around them, empowering them to embrace their inner rhythm and cultivate lasting emotional freedom.

Together, Joshua and Raena Stibal have created *Algorithm of You®* as a revolutionary framework for understanding and mastering emotions, individual algorithmic problem solving styles, and mastering virtues. Through this book, they offer practical tools, reflective exercises, and insightful narratives to help readers recognize, optimize, and refine their emotional responses, ultimately leading to greater self-awareness and fulfillment. Their combined expertise in emotional intelligence, personal development, and strategic thinking makes *Algorithm of You® – Master the flow of your emotions* an essential guide for anyone seeking to unlock their full potential.